HF
5415
.D87
1987

Duro, Robert.

The basic
principles of
marketing warfare

$29.95

DATE			

THE BASIC PRINCIPLES OF MARKETING WARFARE

THE BASIC PRINCIPLES OF MARKETING WARFARE

by
ROBERT DURÖ
and
BJÖRN SANDSTRÖM

Marketing Warfare AB, Sweden

JOHN WILEY & SONS
Chichester · New York · Brisbane · Toronto · Singapore

The Basic Principles of Marketing Warfare by Robert Durö and Björn Sandström
English language edition, Copyright © 1987 by John Wiley and Sons Ltd.
Originally published in Sweden by Liber Förlag © 1985 by
Robert Durö and Björn Sandström and Liber Förlag.

Library of Congress Cataloging-in-Publication Data:

Durö, Robert.
    The basic principles of marketing warfare.
    Bibliography: p.
    Includes index.
    1. Marketing.   I. Sandström, Björn.   II. Title.
HF5415.D87   1987   658.8   87-8317
ISBN 0 471 91545 9

British Library Cataloguing in Publication Data:

Durö, Robert
    The basic principles of marketing warfare.
    1. Marketing
    I. Title   II. Sandström, Björn
    658.8   HF5415
ISBN 0 471 91545 9

Typeset by Acorn Bookwork, Salisbury, Wiltshire
Printed and bound in Great Britain by Biddles Ltd.

Morale relates to physical strength in the ratio three to one. (Napoleon)

Indirect Strategy is just as basic for success in politics and warfare as in sex. In business, the chance of making a killing is much more important than any attempts at influencing people's buying habits directly. (Liddell Hart)

The aim of strategy is to reach a decisive battle by creating and using a situation which undermines the enemy's morale sufficiently to enable him to accept the conditions one wishes to impose upon him. (Beaufre)

All warfare is based on deception. A skilled general must be master of the complementary arts of simulation and dissimulation; while creating shapes to confuse and delude the enemy he conceals his true dispositions and ultimate intent. When capable he feigns incapacity; when near he makes it appear that he is far away; when far away, that he is near. (Sun Tzu, 500 BC)

The Company Strategist

Robert Durö (MBA) has built up, and was in charge of, the Swedish Management Group's strategic training. Over 700 companies have been involved in consultancy and training, among them most of Sweden's successful companies. He was also responsible for the first Western strategic courses in China, involving company heads from seven provinces.

Together with Björn Sandström, he runs the Marketing Warfare AB consultancy.

The Military Strategist

Colonel *Björn Sandström* is head of the Swedish Navy's planning department, with responsibility for short- and long-term development.

He was involved for many years as chief lecturer in strategy at the Military Academy. In business, he has worked as strategic consultant and was involved in the Swedish Management Group's strategy courses. He is also a member of the International Institute for Strategic Studies, London.

Contents

Unlike the military, industry is always at war. If there is peace, they call this a cartel, and as everyone knows, those are not allowed.

(Hans Werthen, chairman of the board of
Electrolux and Ericsson)

Robert Durö and Björn Sandström are jointly responsible for running Marketing Warfare AB, a marketing and efficiency consultancy, whose aims are those of this book. Any queries or observations would be welcomed at the address below:

Marketing Warfare AB
Sandviksvägen 146,
S-162 40 Vällingby, SWEDEN
Tel 08/739 29 88

1 Introduction

In the courses on strategy and company consultancy work in which we have been involved for a number of years, we have found a growing need to understand the principles of marketing warfare. Business today is highly competitive. Far too many companies are having to face the inroads of foreign companies into what are already stagnant markets. Many of them fail to deal with the situation, often for want of a systematic strategy.

Japanese companies, on the other hand, well-known for their deliberate strategy, are continually introducing their products in new market sectors—and in most cases coming to face with competitors who are not in control of strategic interaction. There is no understanding of the aggressor's actions, still less of how to counter them. There is a lack of knowledge of the basic principles of strategy, which makes them fall easily to the Japanese offensive. Japan's success is no coincidence: strategically-minded companies cannot help succeeding in confrontations with strategically ignorant competitors.

This book has been written to give European company managers a basis for understanding, formulating and implementing successful strategies against strategically-minded opponents. The starting point is *classical military strategy*, as described by Carl von Clausewitz, André Beaufre and Liddell Hart. Our presentation does not lay any claim to originality; on the contrary, we have tried our best to follow the basic ideas of strategy as close to their original form as possible.

By way of introduction, we describe and discuss the basics of strategy. André Beaufre's thoughts play a major role in this section, which is natural if one has read his book *Modern Strategy for Peace and War*. In the foreword to the Swedish edition, General Carl-Eric Almgren writes: 'André Beaufre's work is at one and the same time the most complete and the most up to date in the entire field of strategy to be published in our generation.' In Liddell Hart's opinion

1

also, this work is one of the classics of the literature and science of strategy. It is therefore only natural that Beaufre's theories have assumed a prominent place in our work.

In recent times, military thinking has often been linked with commercial marketing strategy. The idea is not new. Military strategic thinking has always been applied in politics and business to a greater or lesser extent. In recent years, the relationship has become much more apparent. There is frequently no distinction nowadays between politics, strategy and economics, which means that military strategic theories can be applied successfully in marketing warfare. Philp Kotler and Ravi Singh, for example, have discussed this relationship in a widely-noted article in the *Journal of Business Strategy*.

This book has been written on the basis of experience acquired during the years that the authors have been involved in strategic planning in business. The starting point was the growing need for strategic thinking in marketing. In autumn 1984, for example, a special course in marketing warfare was held at the Volvo Car Company for all their Swedish managers (1600 in all), based on the contents of this book.

We would like to thank Col Erik Rossander of the Defence College and Col Torbjorn Rimstrand of the Military Academy for their help in formulating strategic and military examples. We would also like to thank Goran Alsterlind, ACO International, for willingly sharing his wide knowledge of marketing warfare.

It is about time that we really understand what the competition is doing and is likely to do, and strike at its weak spots quickly and boldly with our own forces. Strategy can be likened to a mass of water breaking violently through a dam.

The nature of water is that it avoids heights and hastens to the lowlands. When a dam is broken, the water cascades with irresistible force. Now the shape of an army resembles water. Take advantage of the enemy's unpreparedness; attack him when he does not expect it; avoid his strength and strike his emptiness, and like water, none can oppose you. (Sun Tzu, 500 BC)

---

2 What is marketing strategy?

The starting-point of traditional marketing strategy is *the needs of the customer*. Companies strive for profitability and development by giving customers a good product for which a demand exists. This approach is of course the basis of success and will probably be sufficient as long as competition is not too manifest. The problem, however, is that now and in the future companies will be forced to compete for over-established markets. In spite of market segmentation and adaptation to customers' needs, we therefore find a situation in which *a large number of companies are trying to satisfy the same needs*. This is also due, to a large extent, to the rapid development of communications and information systems enabling incursions and competition over geographically extensive markets. In general, the products on offer are all equally good, which means that only seldom do gaps in the market arise where other companies can establish themselves. Putting it crudely, there are too many companies with similar products and too much market communication, with the result that traditional customer-oriented strategy has been partially displaced from its role.

Customer strategy by itself will not therefore be enough to ensure long-term success. Marketing has gradually become *marketing warfare*. In addition to the customer concept, successful strategy must also include how to deal with competitors and other important actors in the market. To achieve positive results, a company must markedly increase its *competitor orientation*. As with customers, competitors must be identified and mapped out. Strategy must be devised so that competitors can be monitored and, where necessary, out-

3

manoeuvred. In a mature market, this is an absolute precondition for survival and success.

The main sub-strategies in marketing strategy can be illustrated as in Figure 1.

Figure 1

In the traditional concept of marketing, customer strategy is *the* dominant strategy. In competition-oriented marketing warfare, the emphasis is on competitor strategy, and great weight is also placed on lateral strategies to create the right conditions for marketing warfare.

In marketing warfare, action against competitors is the decisive factor in ensuring long-term success in marketing. This is therefore the aim of the book. We have not forgotten, of course, that a good customer strategy is needed for success; but customer strategy can be seen as a way of increasing competitiveness. For us, the spotlight is on competition: like Michael Porter, we see both customers and suppliers as potential competitors in the struggle for markets (cf. Porter's theses in his book *Competitive Strategy*, Collier Macmillan, 1981). The theories of strategy should be read with this in mind. Nor does this mean that strategic theories do not apply in other contexts: with a little imagination, they can in fact be applied to practically any sphere of human activity. The basics of classical theory apply wherever we are dealing with a collision of wills, irrespective of whether we are dealing with competitors, customers, people in authority or marital partners.

In strict terms, the art of warfare is divided into *strategy* and *tactics*. Strategy is the overall art of war, on a level with philosophy or psychology. Tactics are the means by which strategy is carried out. We have deliberately avoided putting any great effort into distinguishing between concepts in this book, however. In some cases, we have used the term 'strategy' where, militarily speaking, it would have been more correct to use 'tactics'.

[*Translator's note*: In fact, there are some instances where this has happened, and where the word 'strategy' is not correct in English: in these instances, it has been replaced by 'tactics'.]

3 The basis of strategy

The aim of strategy

The aim of all strategy is to get the enemy where you want him. The main aim for the strategist is to force his will on his opponent. Strategy therefore has a *psychological aim*, which is incredibly important to bear in mind if one wants to understand the real meaning of the term.

Strategic action is always based on power—a fighting potential of some kind. In purely classical strategy, this is made up of armed forces. In more general terms, it can be made up of military, economic, political and psychological factors, which can be combined in practice.

Great care must always be taken in establishing one's fighting potential. Strategic analysis therefore includes a comparison of forces to establish one's relative strength (fighting potential) vis-à-vis one's opponent. Relative strength is an important input value when establishing one's freedom of action in any given situation.

To impose his will on his opponent, a good strategist uses his fighting potential as economically as possible. It is foolish to use ammunition if more simple means will suffice. The best thing, of course, is if the enemy, without realising that influence is being exerted upon him, comes of his own accord to the insight that he should act the way you want him to. Failing this, threats or conflict are resorted to. Rewards and promises can also be used, of course. The decisive factor is that one's opponent accepts what one intends.

The idea of strategy is not infrequently and mistakenly seen as a doctrine with the aid of which one can achieve success in a variety of situations. Such an attitude is not only ignorant but can also undermine the possibility of achieving strategic success.

Strategy—a method of thinking

Strategy should never be reduced to a one-sided doctrine, but is first and foremost a method of thinking, which enables actions and circumstances to be grasped and analysed and viable solutions to problems established.

> *Each different situation demands its own solution—and 'to each situation there therefore corresponds a specific strategy'.* (André Beaufre)

A given rule or strategy may be viable in one situation but inapplicable in another. Throughout history, many mistakes have been made through failure to realize this sufficiently.

At the heart of the concept of strategy is the dynamic interaction which arises out of a conflict of wills. André Beaufre defines strategy as follows:

> *Strategy is the art of grasping and mastering the interaction of wills used as a weapon in settling mutual conflict.*

This definition may appear abstract, but all it really says is that any conflict involves a conflict of wills which is dynamic by nature. Each side is continuously influenced by the other and how it perceives its own situation and that of its opponent. The side that best perceives the collision of wills and masters this interaction will be the victor. As such, strategy and psychology have a lot in common.

If a battle can be won by getting one's opponent to understand that we are 'right' and they are 'wrong', without using any resources, this is of course the best solution of all. Fighting is not an aim in itself, but may be necessary in achieving the goal.

Ways and means

> *The aim is to reach a decisive battle through creating and using a situation which leads to a significant degree of moral collapse in the opponent so as to enable him to accept the will which one wishes to force upon him.* (André Beaufre)

6

The main principle in question is to master the interaction of wills. To be able to grasp the type of interaction correctly, it is essential to establish as quickly as possible which type of conflict of wills is involved. In principle, we distinguish between three types of conflict:

- conflict of preferences;
- conflict of interests;
- conflict of instruments.

Conflicts of preference generally go the deepest, and hence are also the most difficult to deal with. They concern basic values (preferences) which may be ideological, political, religious, economic, etc. Since the aim of strategy is always to get the opponent mentally where one wants him, conflicts where basic values are concerned are particularly difficult to handle. The parties involved often react more ideologically than rationally. There is a great risk that the conflict will lead to large-scale conflict with mutual exhaustion as a consequence. Victory in such a conflict is therefore often dearly bought.

Conflicts of interest deal with strategic interests such as raw material resources, military geography, economics, markets, etc. This is the commonest type of conflict, in both military and marketing terms. The parties involved generally act rationally in this type of conflict.

Conflicts of instrument, finally, are a type of conflict where the parties are agreed as to the goal but have differing opinions as to the means (instruments) of achieving it. This type of conflict may occur between two parties with similar values or common mutual interests; it can also occur internally in an organization and can become quite violent in nature.

The different types of conflict rarely occur in isolation; generally speaking, real conflicts involve elements of all three types. It is therefore a matter of great interest to establish what the important factors are which control one's opponent's actions, so as to get a better opportunity of mastering the conflict of wills.

At the same time, it is important to bear in mind that strategic interaction often concerns more than just two parties. Both in classical military strategy and in fields such as politics or business, there are parties involved other than the main opponents. The interaction of the various wills can therefore be quite complicated.

Wills other than that of the opponent may have a decisive effect: the strategist must therefore grasp and master the psychological situation completely, and not merely focus blindly on the main opponent.

Strategic measures vis-à-vis an opponent are made up of threats, conflict, promises and rewards, frequently in combined form. Measures can be covert or overt. The possession of a strong fighting potential can in itself be a covert threat (or promise) affecting the will of the opponent. Superpowers and large multinational companies are in a much stronger strategic position than small countries or companies. In spite of this, local relationships of forces may be the opposite and give the party which in overall terms is the weaker a good freedom of action. The superpowers, however, can often if necessary mobilize strong forces in fields where they are relatively weak at first. This relationship tends to have a restraining effect on the actions of the other parties.

Allies and neutral parties may play a decisive role in war. Germany lost two world wars in succession because it failed to realize this: it fought wars on two fronts simultaneously, East and West, and drew too many powerful opponents against itself unnecessarily.

Reaching a strategic aim requires *analysis, logic and method*. The conflict of wills must be understood correctly to its full extent. Conceivable solutions must be considered and evaluated so that strategic plans can be established on as viable a basis as possible. Strategy is therefore more a method of thinking than a collection of rules or doctrines capable of being applied in mechanical fashion. Before we take a closer look at strategic thinking, we should take a closer look at classical theories. This is necessary so as to be able to understand what is important in warfare and what is not.

4 Strategic theories

Direct strategy

According to *classical strategy*, the aim should be an accumulation of forces with the aim of annihilating the enemy's main force, so that any remaining forces can be defeated. Battles should be fought between one's own main force and that of the enemy, with the aim of achieving a decisive victory once and for all. This was the strategy which was derived at the end of the 1800s from Carl von Clausewitz's theories, as described in his classic work *Vom Kriege (On War)*, 1834.

In Clausewitz's opinion, victory would be won by:

- use of large-scale force against the enemy's main force (accumulation of forces);
- decisive combat in the main sphere of operations.

According to Clausewitz, the struggle should be waged by alternating defensive and offensive operations. Great importance is attached to defensive tactics, even while preparations are being made for the offensive. Forces should be manoeuvred so as to create the maximum freedom of action at the decisive moment before an all-out offensive is launched. Victory should be achieved through a mighty and, if possible, rapid campaign.

This classical strategy could also be called direct strategy. It was mainly with the help of this strategy that Napoleon won his great victories. Direct strategy has always played a major role in warfare, and dominated European wars in the nineteenth and the first half of the twentieth century. It has sometimes been mistakenly seen as the only classical theory.

Moreover, Clausewitz has not infrequently been misinterpreted. *On War* was not published until after his death, and is not exactly the easiest of works to read. His theories have sometimes been taken to mean that the aim of battle is the physical elimination of the enemy, something which Clausewitz never advocated.

Clausewitz had a clear idea of the psychological aims of war, as can be seen from the following quotation: 'War is an act of violence which seeks to impose our will on the enemy.' This strategy requires ample superiority of forces in the decisive phase. This is simple and straight to the point. There is no idea of misleading the enemy. In the plan of operations, however, a great deal of tactical finesse is required to create the freedom to manoeuvre essential for the decisive battle. Direct strategy must be based on a position of strength if the desired result is to be achieved. If no such position of strength exists, there is a great risk that direct strategy will lead to gigantic trials of force between relatively equal opponents. The deadlock at the end of 1914, the Germans' failure to cross the English Channel after their victories on the continent in 1940 and the Russian campaign in the Second World War are examples of this type of situation.

A decisive battle will only be achieved under these circumstances after a long-drawn-out phase characterized by mutual exhaustion. This is often out of all proportion to the importance of what is at stake, and leads to both victor and loser being totally exhausted at the end of the struggle. Nor will the main aim, that the enemy should also be *mentally* prepared to recognize that it has been beaten, be achieved in this case (cf. Germany in 1918). The battle will have been more a matter of use of resources than of wills.

It can also be seen that this was already true in Napoleon's case, in his inability to solve the problems of England and Russia. Napoleon also came to grief in Spain, where his concept of strategy came up against the indirect methods of querrilla warfare. But Clausewitz and his followers were so blinded by Napoleon's dazzling victories that they were unable to realize that there were limitations; and Clausewitz' strategy undoubtedly does have serious limitations. In many cases, it fails to deal sufficiently with the enemy's will. Only if one is acting from a position of strength and is sufficiently certain of victory can this strategy be recommended uncritically.

Indirect strategy

In contrast to direct strategy, there is *indirect strategy*, which has been given a particularly brilliant exposition by Liddell Hart. The approach of indirect strategy is to work towards victory by using one's forces against weak spots in secondary operational areas. Instead of taking the bull by the horns, as it were, one brings it down by a surprise attack on its weak points. The enemy should be misled, and should not realize what is happening until it is too late. The enemy is enticed away from its strongpoints and into guarding uninteresting sectors, and at the same time an attack is prepared on its weakest points. Attacks may be made in unusual areas, for example, so as to mislead one's opponent and prevent him from seeing the real danger.

According to Liddell Hart, there are six positive and two negative rules, which to some extent go against Clausewitz. Indirect strategy can be summarized in four main principles:

- achieving surprise through the use of unpredictable action;
- using forces against weak spots;
- decisive battles in secondary spheres of operation;
- using indirect methods to force one's opponent to split up his forces.

> *The expert commander strikes only when the situation assures victory. To create such a situation is the ultimate responsibility of generalship. Before he gives battle the superior general causes the enemy to disperse. When the enemy disperses and attempts to defend everywhere he is weak everywhere, and at the selected points many will be able to strike his few.* (Sun Tzu, 500 BC)

Many Allied campaigns during the Second World War bore the marks of indirect strategy. Churchill, who used indirect strategy to a large extent, often looked for Germany's weak points so as to attack them. Early on, for example, he wanted to prevent the Germans from using Norwegian territory. He urged on the invasion of North Africa and was in favour of an invasion via the Balkans instead of in France. Indirect strategy has its limitations, however, when it comes to holding a decisive battle of any great size.

Lastly, let us look at a special form of indirect strategy, namely guerrilla strategy, which is currently the form most in use. Mao Tse-Tung laid down the basics of guerrilla warfare in the following six rules:

- Close cooperation between the population and the guerrillas.
- Retreat when the enemy advances in strength.

- Patrol activities and minor attacks when the enemy withdraws.
- In strategic terms, a ratio of forces of one to five is sufficient.
- In tactical attacks, the ratio should be at least five to one. This ratio is mainly created through what is called the 'centripetal retreat', that is, a united force is recreated during the retreat.
- Where equipment and weapons are concerned, the guerrilla lives from what he takes from the enemy.

The strategy used in Vietnam by General Giap, first against the French, culminating in the victory of Dien Bien Phu in 1954, and then against the United States, illustrates Mao's theses almost perfectly. It does of course require very great sacrifices over a long period of time, but in the end both France and the USA themselves accepted that the fight was over without them being able to achieve their aims. The great powers were defeated by a materially weak but psychologically strong enemy.

Maintaining freedom of action

Whichever strategy is chosen, it should be noted that all actions have a psychological aim: to break the enemy's will to fight and ultimately to make him accept anything one desires. In any fight, there are two separate important elements:

- selecting the *decisive objective* which is to be achieved, taking into account the enemy's strengths and weaknesses;
- selecting *preparatory measures* making it possible to achieve the decisive aims.

Since the other side will be doing likewise, however, the preparatory actions will gradually lead to success for the side which manages to check its opponent's manoeuvres and carry its own through to their end. This is what classical strategy calls 'maintaining freedom to manoeuvre', and is an essential precondition for success in warfare.

> *In this way, the struggle of wills is reduced to a struggle for the freedom to manoeuvre. Each side tries to maintain its own freedom to manoeuvre and at the same time to deny it to its opponent.* (André Beaufre)

By using its forces, the stronger opponent will find it relatively easy to maintain its freedom to manoeuvre against the weaker. The opponent's forces can be tied down while, at the same time, it has the resources to deliver the decisive thrust. This state of affairs is relatively rare, however; it is much more often the case that the two sides are relatively equally matched.

In this case, freedom of action must be created and maintained by superiority in manoeuvring (operations). This means hitting the decisive point at the right time, thanks to the freedom to manoeuvre achieved by creating a sufficiently favourable situation.

> A pitched battle should be fought in the same way as a siege: fire should be concentrated on the decisive point, and as soon as the breakthrough has been achieved, the balance is broken and all else is nothing. (Napoleon)

Victory or defeat depend overwhelmingly on the actions that precede the final battle itself. If the strategy has been good, the ground will have been laid for success. At the same time, operations must be followed through consistently if the goal is to be achieved.

It is for this reason that reserves are kept. These very often account for about a third of the total force, and are sent in at the decisive moment (which Napoleon called the 'climax') to ensure victory.

It is important to use the freedom to manoeuvre achieved and take so much terrain that a good defence can be set up. Clausewitz emphasized the superiority of defence and believed that the justification for attack was to create more favourable conditions for defence.

Operations and battle must have a common aim and be conceived in accordance with what is possible. The course of strategy also applies to the interaction of *wills*, and it is therefore a prerequisite that one must understand the enemy's psyche and understand what defeat would mean to it. All too often, commanders who are skilful in tactical terms have failed to understand this, and victory has been bought much too dearly. Winning a battle is somewhat uninteresting if one loses the war. The aim of war is to make a better peace. No desire for revenge must be created amongst one's opponents. There are many wars and campaigns in history where the long-term result was directly the opposite of that intended. The First World War, for example, did not lead to a stable peace but instead paved the way for the second.

> 'The aim of war is to force one's will upon the opponent.' (Clausewitz)

5 Principles of strategy

Any campaign needs its own strategy, drawn up in the light of the specific situation. Military principles relate to the framework within which we should look for viable strategic solutions. Rules and principles can be of two kinds: either strictly scientific or generally pragmatic and based on experience. Military principles belong to the latter kind: they have grown out of experience in war and are generally valid *irrespective of what strategic principle is applied*. The relative importance of different rules depends of course on the type of operation.

1 Set a goal and stick to it

This first principle is definitely the most important of all. Great care must be taken when establishing war aims. In addition, each phase of the war and each operation must have a more limited aim which must be formulated clearly and simply. Careful consideration in establishing aims will ensure that regard will have been given to probable developments in war so that the aims do not need to be revised. This means that aims must always be *realistic*.

Overall strategic aims are broken down into partial aims for practical use at different levels. The aim must be well grounded in the organization. Tactical leaders must have clearly-defined tasks within the framework of the higher leader's plans. Everyone in the organization must understand how short-term tactical aims tie in with operational and strategic aims. Tactical leaders must be familiar with the tasks of other units and the aims of higher leaders, right up to the overall strategic aim.

The structure (hierarchy) of aims has the outline shown in Figure 2 in principle.

Figure 2

Efforts at all levels must be directed so as to support the aim. Plans and actions must be checked continually to ensure that they lead towards the established aim.

2 *Maintain good morale*

Success in conflict depends more on moral than material factors. Weapons, numbers and other resources cannot make up for a lack of courage, energy, decisiveness or the will to fight. Good morale is therefore vital. *Good leadership* is the most important precondition for achieving this. The importance of leadership is clearly shown by the fact that all successful strategists were also outstanding leaders. They had the ability to inspire their forces and get them to work towards a common aim. Material preconditions such as good equipment, training and adequate organization also of course play an important part where fighting morale is concerned.

The will to fight also depends on to what extent one perceives what one is fighting for as justified and meaningful. Defending one's own country, home and family naturally creates a higher motivation than arcane operations far away in foreign lands. The effect this can have on the will to fight is clearly illustrated by the disciplinary problems of the American army during the Vietnam war.

When the Soviet Union attacked Finland in November 1939, most people expected that Finland would be a walkover for the Russian bear. Things turned out quite differently. Finland withstood the attack in a way that can only be explained by the very high fighting morale on the Finnish side.

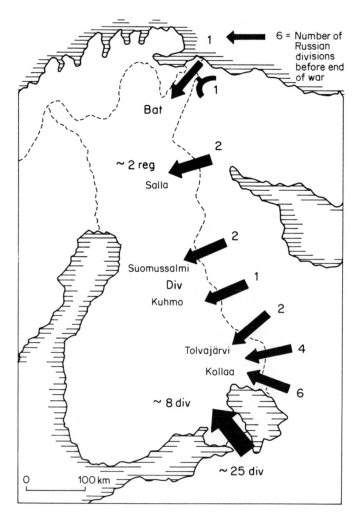

Figure 3. Finnish Winter War, 1939–40

The Finns were fighting for their existence, for their country and their families. Both officers and men were very much aware of this, which strengthened their will and initiative and made tactical success possible in spite of massive Russian superiority.

3 Act aggressively

It is important to take the initiative and act aggressively to win. This does not mean 'attack at any cost'. A defensive attitude is sometimes the right one, but one should never lose any opportunity of regaining

Battle of Trafalgar 1805

Figure 4. Battle of Trafalgar, 1805

the initiative. A successfully aggressive attitude is also important for fighting morale. Put in its simplest form, this rule means that you cannot win a fight without 'cutting out' the other side.

Attack is a method of conflict which should be used in a wide variety of situations. To give the desired result, it must be combined with other factors such as surprise and accumulation of forces. The aim is to get the opponent off balance so that the attack can be aimed at a weak point in his lines. After that, any success will be achieved by force. It is at this point that the accumulated *reserves* should be engaged to achieve a decisive result.

In the battle of Trafalgar in 1805, Lord Nelson gave a good example of what can be achieved with purposefulness, courage, imagination and aggressive morale. By skilfully manoeuvring his forces to windward, gaining a tactically favourable position, it was possible to fight the battle just as the English wanted.

Nelson attacked the enemy by launching his forces in two columns against the enemy lines. In this way, he succeeded in dividing the enemy's forces into three sections, creating confusion and at the same time carrying out an orderly artillery battle from his own side. This aggressive and surprising action involved such tactical advantage that the English won easily in spite of inferior numbers.

4 Aim for surprise/5 Concentrate forces

Surprise and concentration of forces are two important principles which go together with the rule of aggression. Surprise plays a major part in warfare. It has a great effect on morale. Every opportunity should therefore be taken to take the enemy by surprise and avoid being taken by surprise oneself. The principle of concentration of forces is equally important. Success is achieved by a concentration of strength and qualitative superiority over the enemy at the right *time* and *place*.

In an astounding campaign in the spring of 1940, the German army conquered the Dutch, Belgian and French armies and forced the British Expeditionary Force to flee across the Channel. By throwing seven out of ten panzer divisions and the bulk of the air force against the enemy's flank and rear, the preconditions had been created for a rapid breakthrough followed by an attack in depth, encircling the bulk of the Allies' forces and forcing the breathtaking evacuation at Dunkirk.

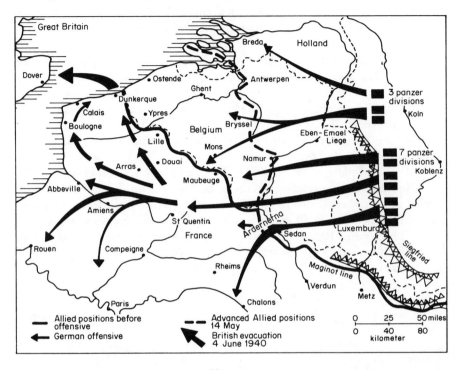

Figure 5

Of course, surprise was also equally achieved by the unexpected choice of the direction of attack, the impenetrable Ardennes, which the French thought unsuitable for mechanized troops and were therefore somewhat neglected in defence plans.

6 Make sure your own forces are secure

Adequate security for one's own forces is essential, since it provides the preconditions for the freedom of action required if aggressive action is to be taken. This means, for example, adequate defence of bases and key terrain.

The need for safety does not justify over-carefulness, however. The main question in war is taking calculated risks. The rule means foreseeing risks and either taking them or eliminating them. Taking

19

risks is not a departure from the rule, but it is a serious mistake not to be aware when taking risks.

The aim of this security is to create the preconditions for the offensive. The rule should not therefore be seen as defensive.

The Allied landings in Normandy in 1944 were an extraordinarily difficult operation. The safety aspects therefore had to be taken into account to a very great extent in both planning and execution. Preparations for this, the largest amphibious operation in the history of the world, were made over a number of years. Total sea and air domination had been achieved. For months, the bombers had attacked lines of communications and defence installations. Detailed measures had been taken to deceive the Germans as to the time and place of the invasion. Artificial harbours would support the operation and enable reinforcements to be brought up. Dummy runs were carried out on exact scale models. Nothing was left to chance. Preparations were highly detailed in all respects. On the day of the invasion, more than 5,000 vehicles and 10,000 planes were used in support of the 150,000-man force which was to be the spearhead against 'Fortress Europe'. The landings were successful; losses were relatively small.

Figure 6. The Normandy landings, 1944

7 Use your forces economically

This rule means balanced use of forces and judicious use of resources with the aim of satisfying the requirements of both accumulation of forces and safety. It does not mean trying to achieve results with as little effort as possible. This is dangerous and in conflict with the rule of accumulation of forces. Economic exploitation means that available forces are used to achieve the maximum possible overall result.

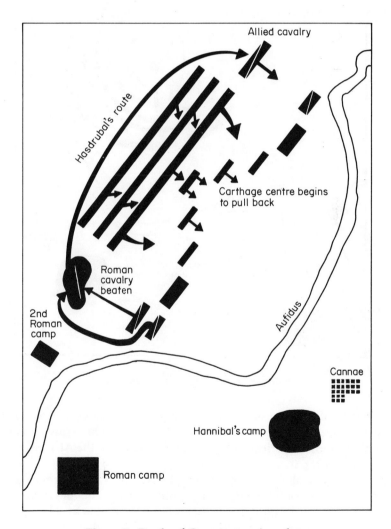

Figure 7. Battle of Cannae, opening phase

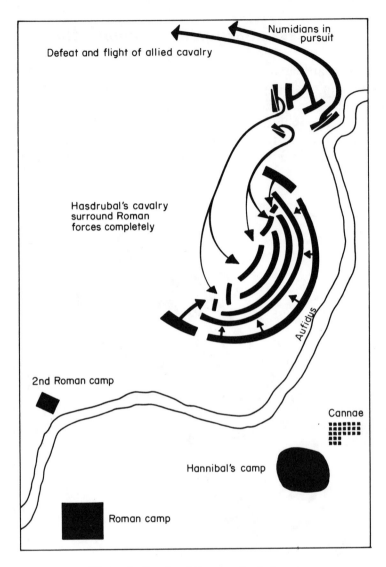

Figure 8. Battle of Cannae, final phase

In the battle of Cannae in 216 BC, Hannibal annihilated a Roman force which was superior in terms of numbers. He drew up his army in a curved line, with his most experienced forces in the centre and the African veterans and cavalry on the flanks.

Hannibal began the battle by driving the Roman cavalry from the field. Then he let the attack by the Roman infantry gain ground and drew his line back in a semi-circle until it was completely bent back. This gave the Romans a false impression of success and channelled the Roman attack into

22

the centre. In the same way, the plan led to the Romans being caught in a dead-end which in turn made decisive victory possible when the African veterans attacked the enemy on both flanks. The battle was completed when the cavalry returned from pursuing the Roman cavalry and attacked the Roman infantry from the rear.

8 Coordination

A campaign must be coordinated to achieve the best results at the least cost. Coordination between different organizations and systems can be achieved either by laying down the chain of command or, where this is not possible to any degree, through cooperation. There must be a readiness to cooperate at all levels of the organization.

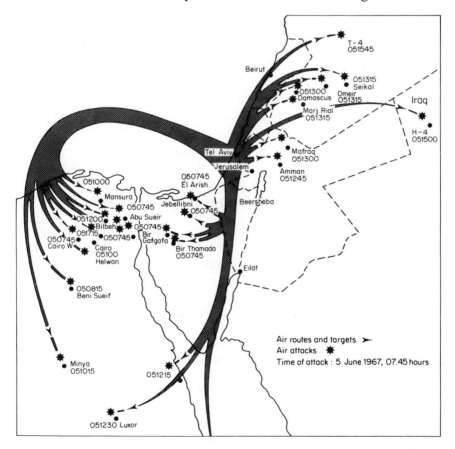

Figure 9. The Six-day War, 1967

By means of a carefully organized and unexpected air attack, the Israelis succeeded in knocking out the Arab air forces on the ground on 5 June 1967. The war was to all intents and purposes won in the first hours. The Arab tank columns could not operate in the desert without air protection. It took six days to bring the war to an end officially, but in fact victory was won in the first half-hour.

9 Try to be adaptable

Warfare requires great adaptability. Plans must be capable of being adapted to changing circumstances and unforeseen events. Rapidly changing situations must be mastered and favourable opportunities used. This requires a flexible intellect, imagination and the ability to take quick decisions on the part of both leaders and their subordinates.

Adequate organization is also essential if the necessary adaptations are to be made. Forces and support functions must be organized to achieve the maximum possible operational freedom. Each leader, for instance, must have control over the support organization to the extent of his operational functions.

In 1973, Syria and Egypt made a surprise attack on Israel. For once, the Israelis were badly prepared. Mobilization had hardly started. To crown it all, the Egyptians unexpectedly succeeded in crossing the Suez canal rapidly, while the scanty Israeli forces in the north were suffering under the massive Syrian tank attack.

The Israelis were forced to depart from their previous battle plans. They had to adapt quickly to the new situation. In the south, they could afford to lose ground. The leaders there largely had to manage with what they had and stay on the defensive until further notice.

In the north, the air force was sent in ruthlessly. On the ground, the tank groups made a sacrificial battle. With a little more daring on the part of the Syrian tank leaders, the situation could have been catastrophic for the Israelis, because, amongst other things, of the proximity to vital parts of Israel. Gradually, however, the Israelis became strong enough to go on to the offensive themselves. Once the Syrians had been driven back and the northern front secured, their forces were quickly diverted to the Sinai front. Here, too, the initiative was gradually regained by crossing the Suez Canal and surrounding a whole Egyptian army. In spite of the unfavourable situation at the beginning, Israel succeeded in mastering the dangerous position through rapid adaptation of its tactics to the circumstances.

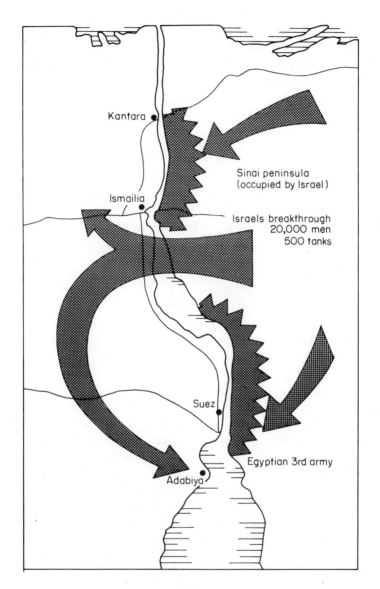

Figure 10. Israel's breakthrough on the Southern front

There is another very interesting aspect of the October war. There were in fact two victors in this war: Israel, to the extent that it was able to stand fast and secure its borders, but also Egypt: for the first time, the Egyptian army had succeeded in beating an Israeli force and retaking parts of Sinai. The feeling of having succeeded on both sides paved the way for a real peace. One could say that the October war was the actual cause of real peace between Egypt and Israel and hence of Sadat and Begin receiving the Nobel Peace Prize.

10 Simplicity

Simplicity is important for successful operations. Clear and simple plans and concise orders reduce opportunities for misunderstanding and confusion. If all else is equal, the simplest plan is to be preferred.

Summary

Let us summarize the ten principles in a military example from the eastern front in the First World War: the battle of Tannenberg in August 1914 (see map, below).

In mid-August 1914, the German front was weakening ominously under the pressure of a powerful and numerically superior Russian offensive. Under the leadership of von Hindenburg and Ludendorff, however, the Germans succeeded in changing the situation and achieving a German victory.

The reason was simply that in spite of the precarious situation they held on to their aim and carried out a counter-strategy which led masterfully to victory. The plan was simple and daring. By taking a calculated risk on the northern section of the front, leaving behind a force (the 1st cavalry division) which was very inferior in numbers but highly flexible against the advancing Russian 1st Army, they succeeded in creating a powerful attack (in terms of time and place) in the south. Coordination of the operation was excellent. Through precise planning and skilful action, they succeeded in warding off the enemy attack and carrying out a surprising counter-attack which radically altered the situation on the eastern front. 50,000 Russians died and 100,000 were taken prisoner. It is difficult to see any faults in the German plan, which stands out as a textbook example of classic military strategy.

The ten basic rules are important, and their importance is also underlined by the fact that they can be found in one form or another

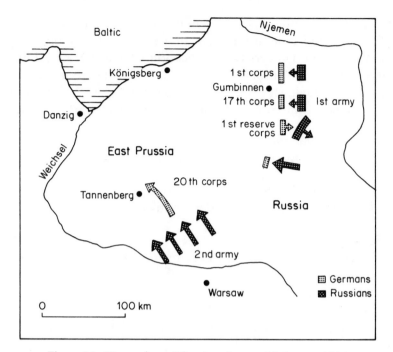

Figure 11. Tannenberg: The situation on 20 August 1914

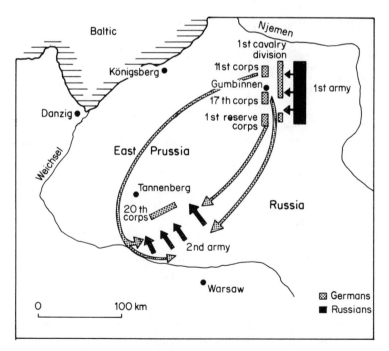

Figure 12. Plan of battle, German 8th Army

in the tactical regulations of the military of all countries. They are also clearly applicable in business. In a seminar article on company economics at the University of Stockholm, in which Ove Liljedahl discussed the applications of the basic rules, he rounded off his discussion by giving examples from Scandinavian Airline Systems (SAS) strategy from managing director (MD) Jan Carlzon's era:

(1) Set a goal and stick to it
SAS: 'We will be the best airline in Europe.'

(2) Maintain good morale
SAS: The personality of the leader; motivation courses.

(3) Act aggressively
SAS: Investing its way out of the crisis in a stagnating market.

(4) Aim for surprise
SAS: While competitors pay 100 million kronor for a new DC9a, SAS repaints and changes the interiors of all its 80 planes for 50 million.

(5) Accumulate forces
SAS: Concentration on profitable European routes.

(6) Make sure your own forces are secure
SAS: Delegated responsibility for results; each unit ensures its own security.

(7) Use your forces economically
SAS: Personnel and fleet tailored to suit the need for resources.

(8) Coordination
SAS: The aim is known and understood by all employees.

(9) Try to be adaptable
SAS: Adaptation to new threats from outside; adapting to deteriorating sales opportunities in the airline industry, advising aircraft manufacturers on how to build modern fleet aircraft.

(10) Simplicity
SAS: Single strategy; instead of getting 100 per cent better on one point, get 1 per cent better on 100 points.

Liljedahl's summary is an example that shows that successful business strategy follows the ground rules of military strategy to a large extent. A number of examples will be presented on the following pages.

6 Battlefield strategy and tactics

Over the course of history, technological change has led to changes in strategy and tactics; but the basic character of conflict is still the same. The elements of conflict are *fire, movement and protection*. These are present in both attack and defence. This applies as much today as it did in the past. Before modern weapons existed, firepower was replaced by the power of the sword, lance or bow. Skills were scarcely technological. The key image of ground warfare was two walls of fighting men pressing against one another. This wall-like formation arose out of the need for each of the combatants to have his flanks and rear protected by his comrades; but this protection only went as far as the flanks, which of course made them the most vulnerable part of the battle line. The weakness of the flanks led to attempts to reach a decisive victory *through outflanking* (surrounding and flank attack) to attack the enemy's flank. This was attained by setting up a more extended front than the other side could achieve. Except in cases where the forces facing one another were more or less evenly matched, this extension of the line led in some places to a weakening of the 'wall'. This meant that there were also opportunities of using the situation by measures aimed at *breaking through* the ranks of the other side and hence creating new, vulnerable flanks.

The aim of conflict is to create confusion in the overall battle order of groups of combatants, and this order is often achieved by outflanking or breakthrough. As soon as the enemy's line is surrounded or broken, their defence is disorganized. The consequent danger for each individual solder involves a psychological shock, which leads in turn to dissolution of the morale binding the fighting soldiers. In other words, the enemy's will to fight is shattered.

30

Such a split and panicking army is generally turned into a rabble. In earlier times, this rabble was an easy victim for the victor. The battle was then transformed into a 'caedes', or massacre, in which the conquered went to the sword while the victor only suffered light losses. A similar situation is also achieved on the modern battlefield when a tank column breaks through and hits deep into enemy lines.

The different manoeuvres can be illustrated in Figure 13.

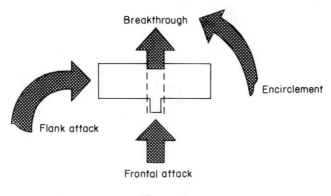

Figure 13

Outflanking (encirclement and flank attack) requires a high degree of flexibility in the battle line. The wings have therefore traditionally been made up of cavalry, and later motorized units or combat vehicles. Breakthrough requires a superior attacking force which needs to be achieved through a considered combination of offensive components. This scheme is also complicated by the fact that the ground for surrounding or breakthrough is often prepared by suitable diversionary or attritive conflict.

The main aim of these preparatory operations is to make a bypass attack and mislead the enemy's forces and to shake their will to fight by fear, fatigue and losses so as subsequently, once the ground has been laid, to assemble one's forces at a decisive point on the wing or centre. The idea behind separate reserves is precisely to create a force for this purpose. *The battle thus is made up of a preparatory phase followed by the decisive phase.*

It is during the decisive phase that the accumulated reserves are sent in to complete success and finally to break the enemy's will to fight.

The art of battle consists to a large extent of the ability to reinforce or maintain a psychological link between one's own troops and to weaken that of the enemy's.

> *The psychological factor is decisive. It is at the base of most creative technical and intellectual processes, from warpaint and battle cries or the whistling bombs of the Stuka dive bombers right up to misleading manoeuvres and surprise to create what Napoleon called the 'climax', where the intrusion will lead to the definitive collapse of the will to fight amongst the enemy.* (André Beaufre)

It is also important that one's tactics should be effective. If possible, one should use the advantage of operating on the so-called 'internal lines'. It is a false economy to make front lines, lines of communications or other communications distances longer than necessary.

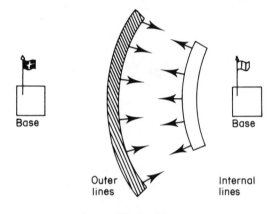

Figure 14

In 48 BC, Caesar had defeated his rival Pompey, but the war now continued against Pompey's supporters. Caesar's position was disputed, and it was therefore a question of reaching a decisive victory once and for all that would ensure the cohesion of the Roman empire. The decisive battle took place at the hostile town of Thapsus in 46 BC.

Thapsus lies on a headland protruding into the Mediterranean. Two necks of land, one on each side of a lake, led out to the headland. Caesar made for the enemy town and besieged it, and expected that the enemy would divide his forces and attempt to trap him between three forces, one on each of the two necks and one in the town. To that extent, Caesar gave up his freedom to manoeuvre, but he ensured it in another way.

His plan was to use the advantages of carrying on the battle on the inner lines and hence creating the conditions for beating the enemy in force, one section at a time. The enemy was to be lured into operating on the outer lines and hence would be unable to parry Caesar's locally massive counter-attack. The enemy fell into the trap.

32

Leaving a small besieging force at the town and a weak delaying force on the southern neck, Caesar collected the majority of his forces against the enemy on the northern neck (1). With this enemy out of the way, Caesar followed with a smaller force, at the same time rapidly switching his main force to the southern neck and attacking the enemy there. This enemy, too, was defeated (2), after which Caesar was now able to continue round the lake and cut off the retreating enemy in the north (3). The victory was complete.

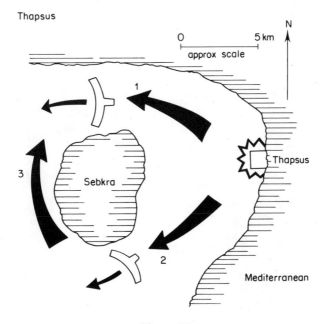

Figure 15

FERMENTA

One company operating distinctly on the internal lines is the Swedish company Fermenta. The company manufactures semi-finished products for the pharmaceutical industry. It mainly produces base penicillin, generated biologically. Fermenta's business concept is based on forward-looking integration in the processing chain and diversification of the product range. From mainly producing base products, the company intends to extend production of intermediate products and active substances. The aim of increased integration is to ensure outlets, improve infrastructure, stabilize prices and improve flexibility. They are trying to operate on the inner lines. Continued integration is achieved largely through company takeovers and joint ventures.

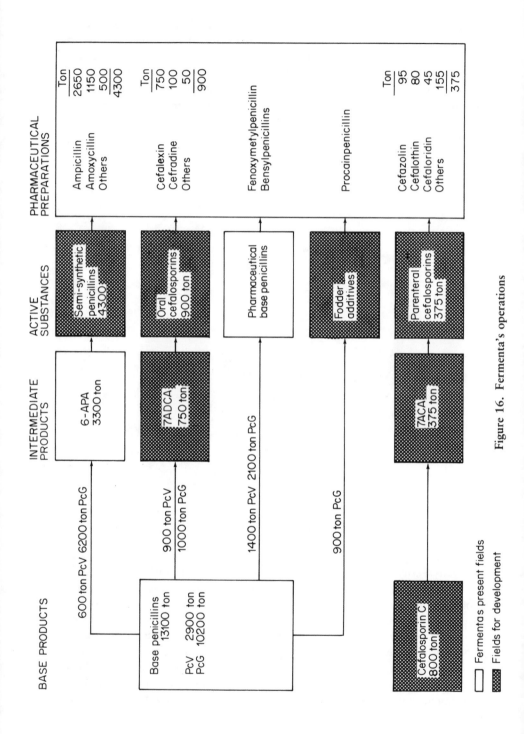

Figure 16. Fermenta's operations

34

Note: Fermenta got into financial problems in 1986/87; not because their strategy was wrong, but because it was poorly executed.

ATLET

The Swedish company Atlet is another company operating on the internal lines. It builds, processes and markets electric fork-lift trucks and on-line-based warehouse management systems for the European market. The company's turnover in 1984 was 253 million kronor, and it had 470 employees.

Atlet uses the Boston model (see p. xxx) in choosing the right products; in other words, using large-scale production, giving advantages of scale for the various company functions and reduced warehousing costs. The company standardizes components used in the various types of truck to reduce warehousing and servicing costs. It is reducing production times for machines and working rhythms, which enables production in short series which in turn leads to reduced stockholding. Production is guided by the Japanese KANBAN philosophy, which involves minimum interim storage. Purchasing is guided by the Japanese 'just in time' philosophy, which means reduced warehousing costs.

Successful tactics on the battlefield very often involve large use of indirect methods. These methods consist not in 'taking the bull by the horns'; in other words, in not engaging the enemy in a direct trial of strength, but only engaging him after he has been disturbed, surprised and unbalanced by attacks from unforeseen quarters. In the same way, the indirect method is forced on whichever of two opponents is not sure of being strong enough to beat the enemy in a battle on terrain chosen by the opponent. Liddell Hart has rightly pointed out that one is never sure of being sufficiently strong, and even if one is, victory may be bought too dearly.

The indirect method can also be extended from the field of tactics to strategy as such. The first factor in indirect strategy is to establish the margin of freedom of action offered by the situation and to ensure the possibility of maintaining or if possible extending this margin, while reducing the corresponding margin for the enemy as far as possible.

It is therefore a question of creating the maximum freedom of action before the battle. This cannot be done solely by manoeuvring in relation to the battlefield, but it is just as important to act outside it. Liddell Hart has emphasized the importance of lateral manoeuvres. Freedom of action must be established 'globally', even if the war is local. Success therefore depends to a large extent on how well we succeed in acting on the 'world' level. Lateral manoeuvres are often of decisive importance in making success possible.

The concept of lateral manoeuvres

The main idea of lateral manoeuvres is to ensure the maximum freedom of action by paralysing the enemy with a number of different deterrent measures outside the actual area of conflict itself. André Beaufre emphasizes that this is a matter of psychological manoeuvring, in which one tries by any means possible to achieve the same effect: political, economic, diplomatic and military. The methods used can range from the most subtle to the most brutal. One may appeal for respect for the law, both national and international. One may appeal to moral or human values, or try to create a bad conscience in the mind of the opponent by getting him to doubt the

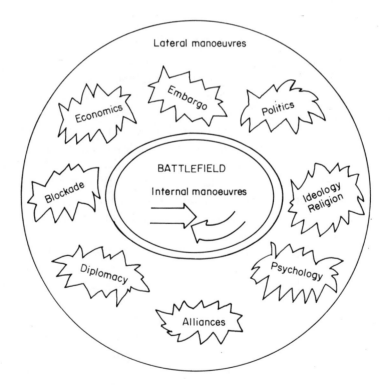

Figure 17

rightness of his cause. One can try to create an opposition in his own country, while also seeking to stir up international opinion.

The aim of strategy is the starting-point for strategy in lateral manoeuvres. It is a question here of creating a real psychological plan of operations, constructed in accordance with the same strict rules as for a plan of operations in the field of strictly military strategy.

Lateral manoeuvres are a central part of all indirect strategy; in marketing too, great attention must therefore be paid to them.

VOLVO

Volvo group chief Pehr Gyllenhammar had long been advocating an upgrading of the motorway network from Oslo to the continent (Scandinavian Link). When, in 1984, the Social Democratic government decided that the Uddevalla shipyard should be shut down, the commercial life of an entire area was threatened. The government was forced to take proper measures, not least in view of the coming elections in autumn 1985.

In January 1985, Volvo decided to build a new car factory for 40,000 cars a year in Uddevalla, on the west coast of Sweden about 70 km from Gothenburg—an investment of 1.5–2 billion kronor. At the same time, the government decided that a motorway should be built between Uddevalla and Gothenburg (part of the Scandinavian Link). Volvo would receive local grants of at least 200 million kronor, and permission over the next few years to use investment funds totalling 12.5 billion kronor. Since Volvo's application related not only to present but also to future allocations to the investment fund, Volvo pushed its tax problem into the future. The Swedish journal *Business World* thought that this was where the greatest profits for Volvo would lie.

What the head of Volvo did was to use lateral manoeuvres to increase Volvo's freedom of action and fighting potential within the fight for market segments in (above all) the car and goods vehicle war.

IBM

IBM's competitors found themselves truly knocked out by its offensive which started with the introduction of third generation computers (the 360 series), and started to bring legal actions against IBM for breach of monopoly regulations, restriction of competition, and so on. They tried to move the struggle from the battlefield, where they were always losing to IBM, to the courts so as to get the courts and general public opinion to turn against IBM (lateral manoeuvres). IBM engaged some of the USA's most skilful lawyers and succeeded in getting a court ruling in its favour.

The competitors began to despair. Then, suddenly, something happened.

In 1972, IBM started its 'SMASH' campaign which in all respects, including the choice of name, was constructed along military lines. SMASH involved a 25 per cent reduction of lease prices, a massive sales offensive and indications to competitors that IBM did not intend to renew their licences.

Telex, which made peripheral equipment, took IBM to court in Tulsa (where they did not like East Coast companies). The complaint was the old chestnut: *IBM had monopolized or tried to monopolize the production, sale and leasing* of peripheral equipment *by means of unjust marketing and pricing policies.* Telex's claim was for $416m. IBM countered by charging Telex with infringement of patents and theft of industrial secrets.

Judgment was given on 14 September. Both sides were found guilty of the charges. IBM was ordered to pay compensation of $3 \times \$350m$ to Telex, and was ordered to change its marketing activities. Within a few days, writs against IBM were flooding in from its competitors.

The competitors thought that they had found a weak spot in 'fortress IBM'. In 1975, the judgment of the court was reversed, and now it was Telex which had to pay compensation, which would mean economic ruin. IBM and Telex therefore came to an amicable settlement. IBM's competitors withdrew their writs and in other cases amicable settlements were also reached. With the help of the most skilful lawyers in the United States, 'fortress IBM' had won the *lateral manoeuvres* in the same crushing way as they had won the battles on other fields.

(SOURCE: *IBM, Colossus in Transition*, Robert Sobel, Times Books)

CHRYSLER

The acute problems of Chrysler in 1978, when it lost $205m, came as no surprise to those engaged in the car industry. At the time of the first oil crisis in 1973, Chrysler, like General Motors and Ford, had a pile of hard-to-sell gas-guzzlers on its hands. When the market changed, and demand for medium and large cars disappeared overnight, Chrysler did not have enough cars, and those that were being produced were of poor quality. In fact, quality was so poor that Chrysler was forced to extend the warranty on new cars to 12,000 miles before people would even risk buying its cars.

When Lee Iacocca, the Vice-President of Fords, was 'given the push' by Henry Ford II in 1978, he was offered the job of VP at Chrysler, with the promise of becoming president within a year. In his best-selling book *IACOCCA*, Iacocca writes that if he had known the problems awaiting him, he would never have taken the job at Chrysler.

He could not have been completely unaware of the problem, particularly as Hal Sperlich, his good friend since the days at Ford and the chief designer of the Ford Mustang, was in full swing developing Chrysler's K cars (Reliant, Aries). Unless the K cars came up trumps, Iacocca would have a hard job succeeding in his 'lateral manoeuvres' of 1979 of going to Congress for help.

When the second oil shock came at the beginning of 1979, Chrysler's financial situation became completely untenable. In the situation, Chrysler in fact had no choice but to go to Congress and ask for help. There was an uproar when Chrysler asked for $1.5 billion in Federal loan guarantees. The critics were vehement that it was a part of the rules of capitalism that companies flowered and went under—the 'survival of the fittest'. To intervene in this process was against the basic principles of free enterprise itself.

Iacocca shuttled between Highland Park and Washington to explain to Congressmen and journalists that Chrysler's problems had largely been created by Federal legislation and regulations which had hit Chrysler particularly hard, since it was much smaller than General Motors (GM) or Ford and hence had significantly fewer cars over which to spread the fixed conversion costs. But Iacocca's words seemed to fall on deaf ears. Congress thought that it was Chrysler's poor company management which was the cause of all its problems.

Finally Iacocca said, 'Okay, let's stop this crap. It's fifty percent your fault and fifty percent our fault, because I know all the management sins. What do you want me to do? Crucify the guys who aren't there? They made mistakes. Now let's get back to the matter at hand: you guys helped us to get into this mess.'

The US Treasury Department had made a study which estimated that bankruptcy for Chrysler would cost the US 2.7 billion dollars in the first year alone in terms of redundancy money and social security payments, so Iacocca continued: 'You guys have a choice. Do you want to pay the $2.7 billion now, or do you want to guarantee loans of half that amount with a good chance of getting it all back? You can pay now or you can pay later.'

Iacocca then set his staff to working out how many people in each state and district depended directly or indirectly for their livelihood on Chrysler remaining on the market. Then they sent the frightening figures out to their subcontractors and sales dealers so that together they could put pressure on Congressmen and local politicians.

From the statistics on Federal help which were given to various companies during the course of the year, Iacocca got Congress to understand that Chrysler was not the only company which had asked for and got help. He also showed all the steps that were being taken internally within Chrysler to get out of the crisis. But the more the public read about the crisis at Chrysler, the less cars Chrysler sold: for who was prepared to buy a car from a company where you didn't know if it would still be there when you needed services or spares? Something drastic had to be done, and quickly. Chrysler's advertising agency, Kenyon & Eckhardt, thought: 'The situation is critical, and you've got a choice. You can die quietly, or you can die screaming. We recommend that you die screaming. That way, there's always the chance somebody will hear you.'

Chrysler decided to go on to the counter-attack. The message was to be twofold:

- Chrysler had no intention of giving up, but would go on fighting in the automobile industry.
- Chrysler made the type of car which America really needed.

In its advertising, Chrysler put questions such as: 'Would America be better off without Chrysler?' 'Isn't Chrysler building the wrong kind of cars?'

The advertising campaign helped Chrysler sell cars and gradually get the support of Congress for Chrysler's request for loan guarantees. It also raised morale amongst Chrysler employees, suppliers and dealers. United Auto Workers (UAW) chairman Douglas Fraser worked just as hard as Iacocca to get Congress to come up with the loan guarantee, and his friendship with Vice-President Mondale certainly did no harm.

President Carter was favourable towards Chrysler and was also a great admirer of Chrysler's newspaper and TV advertising, which imprinted on people's consciousness a picture of the little company fighting for its existence in a hostile world. Congress finally voted through Chrysler's loan guarantee by 271 votes to 136, and Lee Iacocca eventually got his ammunition for continuing the fight for Chrysler's survival. For its part, the United States had a new legendary hero.

(MAIN SOURCE: *Iacocca*, Lee Iacocca, Bantam Books)

Direct manoeuvring

Once lateral freedom of action has been established, there is still the need to create operational freedom of action on the battlefield. We call this 'direct manoeuvring'. Beaufre emphasizes that the problem in this respect concerns three variable but mutually complementary factors: *material resources*, *reserves of morale* and the *time factor*. If the material resources far outweigh those of the enemy, reserves of morale can be less and the manoeuvring very short. If, on the other hand, material strength is low, this must be made up for by very strong morale and manoeuvring becomes a long-term process.

In the field of operations, the main aim of strategy is to reach a *quick decisive battle* or, if time allows, to reach the decisive stage in a *struggle of attrition*. Rapid operations are of course to be preferred if success is sufficiently certain. This is exceptional, however. More often one is forced to operate towards successive partial aims. The extreme form of this Beaufre calls *artichoke tactics*.

Artichoke tactics

Artichoke tactics aim at using local superiority to realize very rapidly a partial aim within the limits of the freedom of action available, and then to go on to the next partial aim, and so on. The main reason for success is that one achieves freedom of action through lateral manoeuvres. The aim must also appear to be sufficiently limited for it to be acceptable to one's opponent and to international opinion.

Initially, Hitler was very successful in presenting each and every one of his successive aims as the only one and the last one. This gamble paid off three times in a row up to the Munich crisis, but after Prague (March 1939), people were no longer deceived by his artichoke tactics.

It should be pointed out that because of their violent and sensational character, these artichoke tactics are often much more dangerous to deal with than a strategy of attrition.

Attrition

The *second extreme form of lateral manoeuvring* tries to achieve an aim, sometimes of great importance, less with the aid of military victory than through keeping up a drawn-out conflict, designed and organized to become more and more exhausting for the enemy. This is the *strategy of attrition*, often assisted by guerrilla strategy, which has Mao Tse-tung as its main theorist and most successful practitioner.

The idea of manoeuvring through attrition is an interesting one. In many respects it is very cunning. The idea is to get a significantly stronger opponent to accept what we want. The strategy must be designed so as not to give him the opportunity of using his superiority. To achieve this, the aim is only to use extremely limited resources against him. Inferiority in military terms must be made up for by a growing superiority in terms of morale, since the campaign will be very drawn out. In this way, operations develop on two different levels simultaneously: on the level of material forces and, where psychological operations are concerned, on the level of morale.

On the *material level*, the main thing is to hold out. If one is greatly inferior in terms of physical resources, one can only survive by

41

refusing to engage in open conflict and at the same time using a pinprick strategy to keep the conflict alive at a low level. This generally points to *guerrilla actions*.

There are two principles which are used to ensure the guerrilla's freedom of action.

- *The first* aims at frightening the population from doing anything for the enemy.
- *The second principle* is to stretch the threat to the enemy to its fullest extent, without forcing the enemy to withdraw. In this way, one forces on him an increasingly serious problem of ensuring that he is sufficiently well protected.

The application of the latter principle means that the enemy is forced to sacrifice significant forces to guarding a growing number of points, which it it succeeds to any great extent makes it possible to compensate for the actual balance of forces between the two sides.

On the *psychological level*, the main principle is also to be able to hold out, to develop and maintain morale at its highest level among both the fighting forces and the population. The backbone of morale, the will to fight, is as such the decisive element for success.

Irrespective of whether the strategy is aimed at a short or long war, the indirect method is important in achieving success. Only very seldom is the ratio of forces such that direct strategies or methods can be applied in isolation.

Counter-strategies

After the First World War, indirect strategy came into use to an increasing extent, mostly with successful results. In devising counter-measures against such an attack, it is necessary more than in any other field to distinguish what is important from what is not. In direct strategy, forces are the essential thing: that is, the material or economic means whose size enables freedom of action to be gained more or less easily. In indirect strategy, the main thing is to use psychological means to create one's own freedom of action and limit that of one's opponent. Interest here is centred on looking for the indirect means that make this possible. The aim should be to block one's opponent's opportunities of acting, to frighten him off from acting through both direct and lateral manoeuvres.

On the *psychological level*, the most important element of the potential to frighten, as far as lateral manoeuvres are concerned, is to be able to display a united front of like-minded parties who have banked their prestige on blocking the opponent. Prestige is a composite function of actual power and effectiveness and of present opinions of future power and effectiveness.

In geographical terms, one must select the areas where one intends to take up a position, in the form of either defence, threat or attack. This choice should be aimed partly at the areas which protect your sensitive points, partly at those which constitute a threat to the enemy's vulnerable points and if possible those where intervention should be easy and economical to carry out.

> *The general who can assess the value of ground manoeuvres his enemy into dangerous terrain and keeps clear of it himself. He chooses the ground on which he wishes to engage, draws his enemy to it, and there gives battle.* (Sun Tzu, 500 BC)

In the case of a violent attack of the type which occurs in some of the phases of 'artichoke tactics', one should have the tactical forces to be able to prevent a rapidly executed *fait accompli*. The tactical presence of such forces will normally be used to create an effective deterrent where internal manoeuvring is concerned. If, on the other hand, one does not have the required means on the spot, one is forced initially to turn to lateral manoeuvres.

In the case of an indirect attack of the 'attrition strategy' type, a number of solutions are available. The best, if possible, is to protect the essentials (e.g. existing government controls), without engaging resources of any size in secondary fields, and then dealing with the conflict by stifling it through sufficiently effective lateral manoeuvring. If this lateral manoeuvring is not possible, however, one is forced to undertake direct manoeuvring aimed at a direct counter-offensive. Such an operation is always risky, however, and this is something one should be fully aware of.

7 The content of strategy

Strategic action uses lateral and direct manoeuvring. The aim is to impose one's will on one's opponent, that is, the competition. At the same time, we have to withstand the attacks of the competition. This requires good fighting morale in the organization. We can summarize the principal contents of strategy in the following formula, borrowed from André Beaufre:

$$S = uMPT$$

In this formula—the general strategic formula—'u' is the unique factor in the case in question, 'M' is the material and economic forces involved. 'P' the psychological forces and 'T' the time factor. In direct *strategy*, the material forces involved are predominant, while 'P' is not as significant and 'T' is relatively small. In *indirect* strategy, the relative importance of the variables is reversed, and 'P' becomes the dominant factor.

The choice of strategy—direct or indirect—depends on the circumstances. We will return to this point later, but even at this stage we can note that indirect strategy is very frequently superior if one is not certain of success. Liddell Hart expressed this as follows:

> "Indirect strategy is as much the basis for success in politics and warfare as in sex. In business, the feeling that there is a capture to be made is much more significant than any attempt to influence purchasing directly."

We could say that in indirect strategy, intelligence replaces physical force. But this does not mean that we should forget that the involvement and application of *material forces remains an absolute precon-*

44

dition in indirect strategy also. Material fighting potential must always be sufficiently available for both direct and indirect strategy to be successful.

Fighting potential and comparison of forces

Fighting potential is the power base for strategic action. It includes not only material/economic and military, but also political and psychological factors. It will be readily seen that building up armed forces as a basis for action is an essential part of military strategy. What is not so readily apparent is that this build-up must apply equally to the political and psychological elements of the fighting potential.

In the war for markets, power bases are built up on material and psychological factors. A certain economic potential is always necessary. It is essential to have a good product which one believes in. The organization must be sufficiently well constructed and must have the will to fight.

Fighting potential thus has a very great influence on the opportunities for strategic action. For this reason, strategic decision-making processes, which we will discuss in Chapter 12, always include analysis both of one's own strengths and weaknesses as well as those of the competition. The aim of this analysis is to establish one's fighting potential vis-à-vis the competition and hence one's freedom to act.

Assessing one's fighting potential and making a comparison of forces is a difficult art, since so many different factors are involved. The factors also vary between the competition and ourselves. In military terms, it may, for example, be a relatively simple matter to compare numbers of combat vehicles; but even this can lead to problems, since the performance of combat vehicles varies considerably. Then there are also such difficult-to-measure factors as level of training, fighting habits and fighting morale.

It is obviously not enough simply to compare numbers of combat vehicles. One side may have anti-tank weapons which neutralize the other side's superiority in numbers of combat vehicles. Other types of unit may be decisive, for example if the terrain is unsuitable for mechanized units. Artillery and air support may be decisive in certain situations, fieldworks and defensive preparations in others.

Military comparison of strength must cover *total operational*

45

effectiveness at a given time and a given terrain, taking into account all types of fighting forces as well as support, maintenance and the will to fight.

To enable this problem to be solved as methodically as possible, some form of operational unit is used enabling different units of forces to be converted to a common quantity. In Swedish military evaluation, the unit of a 'large battalion' is used, which is not a unit as such but a fictive unit used to describe operation forces. The comparison of strength is carried out once one has converted real units (e.g. tank divisions, infantry brigades, reserve units) to 'large battalions'.

In marketing warfare, total operational forces must be assessed and compared in the same way. This can be said to be covered by the following key words:

- Product (e.g. quality, characteristics, packaging, service).
- Place (e.g. distribution channels and geographical location).
- Price (e.g. list price, discounts, credit).
- Promotion (e.g. advertising, personal sales, PR activities).
- Personnel (organization, skills, fighting morale).
- Positioning (vis-à-vis customers, competitors and others).
- Politics (degree of lateral freedom of action).

Traditional methods such as WOTS-up analysis (Weakness, Opportunities, Threats, Strength) are good for resource inventories only if one takes dynamics into account. It is a question of creating a synthesis and being able to compare forces in terms of time and space.

Strategic interaction, as we said earlier, is dynamic. Comparison of strengths must take account of this, In any given market, fighting potential will vary over time in the same way that military forces may vary over time in a particular section of terrain. Let us illustrate this with a simple military example.

In a terrain where a decisive battle is sought (shown by a circle in Figure 18?), there is initially our battalion A (assessed at 2 large battalions on this terrain), and the enemy regiment D (assessed at 4 large battalions). The enemy therefore starts off from a position of superiority, but not to the extent that he can beat us in a short time.

However, the enemy can concentrate considerable forces in the area where he brings his division E (assessed at 12 large battalions).

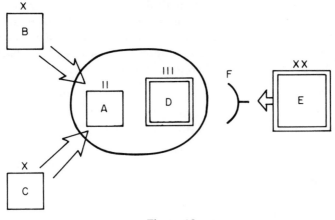

Figure 18

Our delaying force F, however, is estimated to be capable of delaying the division's advance for at least a week.

We can send in brigade B (assessed at 6 large battalions) within two days and brigade C (assessed at 4 large battalions) in three days.

The comparison of strength for the next ten days is therefore as in Figure 19.

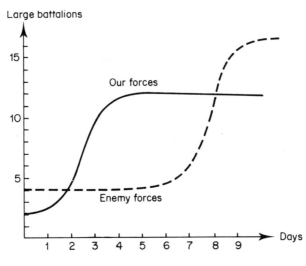

Figure 19

This comparison shows that although the enemy is superior in total terms (16 large battalions to 12), we can create a local superiority and beat his regiment D. From the third day onwards, we can achieve such a local superiority of forces that we can go onto the attack (12 large battalions to 4). The decisive battle must therefore be sought before day seven.

In the same way, comparison of forces in the marketing war must be made in terms of time and place. The aim is to establish our freedom of action and hence create a basis for evaluating the competition's freedom of action and what our options are. One way of carrying out the comparison could be as follows:

(1) Begin by defining the competition and the battlefield (market sector).
(2) Put the success factors in the market in order of importance (KFS—key factors of success).
(3) Define the time scale and at what time the evaluation will be made.
(4) Define your own company's strength, and that of your competitors, at that point in time. Collect the results in a table: this might look like Table 1.

Table 1

Comparison factor	Weight	Our strength			Comp. strength		
		Now	2 yrs	5 yrs	Now	2 yrs	5 yrs
Product quality	0.3	2	5	8	5	4	3
Service	0.2	4	5	6	5	5	5
Distribution	0.2	4	5	6	5	5	5
Price	0.1	5	5	5	4	4	4
Image	0.1	4	5	6	6	5	4
Sales organization	0.1	4	4	5	5	5	5
Sum (points × weighting)		3.5	4.9	6.4	5.0	4.6	4.2

Putting this into diagram form gives the result in Figure 20.

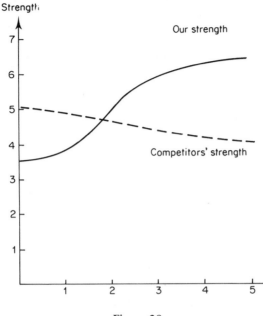

Figure 20

The comparison can also take the form of a competitive profile analysis. This method is often particularly suitable at the tactical/operational level. Using the competitive profile analysis, let's see how we can go about comparing strengths between ourselves and a number of competitors, at both company and product levels.

(1) We begin by defining which competitor we want to compare ourselves with.
(2) Then we write down the factors which account for our success and that of the competitor in the market (key factors of success—KFS).
(3) The factors are then placed in order of importance, the most important factor first.
(4) Now it is time to write in our position relative to the competitor chosen.

The picture we get of our own fighting potential and that of the competition at company level or in the strategic business unit (SBU) may look like Figure 21.

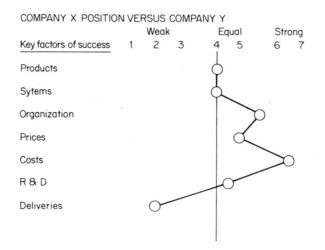

COMPANY X POSITION VERSUS COMPANY Y

Figure 21

We then repeat the procedure for the other competitors.

Now we have a good idea of our overall strength, it is time to use the competitive profile analysis at product level in the way described above. The picture we get of our own strength and that of the competition at product level may look like Figure 22.

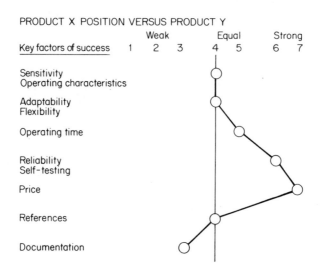

PRODUCT X POSITION VERSUS PRODUCT Y

Figure 22

The comparison of strengths we have made at company and product level is a statistical comparison. Taking the time factor into account, and weighing up the competition's probable steps and our own planned ones, we can describe the expected situation at company and product level for (say) 12 months as Figures 23 and 24.

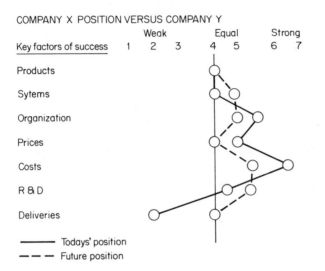

Figure 23

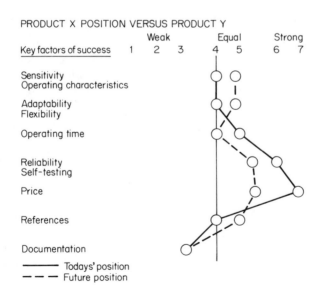

Figure 24

Positioning

The first step in the strategic marketing war is to position your product so that the starting-point for the offensive is as good as possible. In this sense, positioning can be seen as a part of building up fighting potential. Al Ries and Jack Trout have developed a positioning strategy for marketing warfare in their book *Positioning: the Battle for Your Mind*. Their main message is as follows:

(1) *Create a psychological fighting potential. Position the product mentally in the consciousness of customers and competitors.*
To achieve this, you have to break through the invisible protective walls surrounding people today who are literally swamped by information. People have a very limited capacity to deal with information. It is therefore a question of making the message very hard-hitting and differentiating yourself from other similar information so that it penetrates into people's consciousness.

In achieving this, there is a great advantage in being first on the market with the product you are launching. Nothing can in fact replace the enormous advantage this involves.

It is also a question of going whole-heartedly when you have introduced your product; otherwise there is a risk that someone else will take over the idea and succeed in getting it off the ground before you have captured enough key terrain (market segments) for a successful defence to be possible. Ries and Trout sum this up in the thesis: 'The firstest with the mostest!'

(2) *Create an insuperable impression. Convince competitors that counter-attack is meaningless without comprehensive preparations and build-up of forces.*
Everything possible must be done to create the desired impression of strength. The best thing, of course, is to really be the market leader, and this is naturally the thing to aim for. Very often, however, total market domination cannot be achieved for either the product or the market. In this case, the aim should be to hit the segment where you can be number one. 'It is better to be a big fish in a little pool than a little fish in a big pool', as a Chinese saying goes. The strength of being number one is in fact so overwhelming that if you succeed here you can hardly fail as long as your defence strategy is at all realistic. Getting to the top is hard; staying there is very often quite easy.

(3) *Use aggressive tactics with a high degree of indirect methods to position the product rapidly on the market.*
'In love and war, everything is permitted.' Remember it is better to make a mistake than not to do anything at all. Ries and Trout summarize this as 'Anything worthwhile doing is worthwhile doing lousy. If it wasn't worthwhile doing, you shouldn't have done it at all.'

Some of the more important aspects of positioning tactics are as follows:

- Look for gaps—*market sectors* forgotten by the competition.
- Establish a *hard-hitting* product name. Choose a name which says what sort of product it is. *New product—new name*. Avoid extending an already-established name to a new product. Ries and Trout call the trap that you can fall into otherwise the 'Line Extension Trap' and show that this is one of the main shortcomings in marketing.
- *Reposition the competition.* Compare yourself with a known competitor, and change consumers' images of competing brands.

Take Beck for example (a brewery), comparing itself with Lowenbrau on the US market: 'You've tried the most popular German beer in the USA (Lowenbrau): now try the most popular German beer in Germany (Beck's).' This worked, since consumers had an image of Lowenbrau which was wrong.
Raphael (aperitif) compared itself with Dubonnet in the following way: the ad. showed a bottle of Raphael—'Made in France'—and a bottle of Dubonnet—'Made in USA'. The text read: 'For $1 less, you can enjoy the imported bottle.'
The shock was reading that Dubonnet is made in America and not in France.

- Market *aggressively*. Avoid comparisons with similar, well-established products. It is sometimes more appropriate to talk about what a product is not rather than about what it is. The first car was called a horseless carriage. Off-road motorbikes, lead-free petrol, low-calorie soft drinks are some examples of marketing a product for what it isn't.

Avis said they were not the biggest in their ad: 'Avis is only No. 2 in car hire, so why hire from us? Yes: we try harder!'

- Create a position nobody else wants.

Volkswagen marketed itself in the US with the following message: 'The 1970 VWs will stay ugly longer!'

- *Keep your message simple*. The average consumer can only deal with up to 7 competing brands. A simple message can help you be one of those 7.
- Avoid company names which only consist of initials. It is OK to shorten International Business Machines to IBM in marketing, since everyone knows IBM, but it would be completely wrong to introduce Marketing Warfare AB abbreviated to MW AB. You have to be really well known before you can abbreviate the name of your company.
- Don't forget, either, that it can be enough to cooperate with competitors to create sufficient fighting potential. We will deal with this later, however.

8 Predicting the future

The greatest difficulty with the art of war is its *variability*. To create successful strategy, it is therefore a question of predicting and adapting strategy in line with these changes. Innovation carries an obvious risk; but sticking to routine is often a lost cause in advance.

Beaufre states that strategy must avoid building on the basis of rigid and risky hypotheses of the kind advocated here and there by operations analysts. Calculations of probability are no substitute for strategy: strategy is far too complicated and psychologically oriented for that. Instead, it should be based on a number of *options*. These should be future-oriented and of a breadth ensuring long-term freedom of action.

This requirement means that one should place the emphasis on well-equipped organizations for intelligence operations and defence research.

Only in exceptional cases has a military commander of genius—Napoleon stands out here as an example—been able over a long period of time to acquire any great superiority through his way of analysing the situation and forming a strategy completely superior to that of his opponents. But precisely this superiority leads in the end to the opponents learning to adapt their actions to the new conditions, and after some years the game becomes more equal.

> One of the most important factors in classical military strategy has always been the ability to grasp the changing conditions of warfare faster than one's opponents and hence being in a position to foresee the effect of the new factors. (Beaufre)

But new formulae claiming to be clearly capable of solving difficulties have always had a relatively short-lived effect. Conditions are changing continually, and it is therefore a question of not losing strategy in rigid doctrines which are soon outdated.

The main key to the future therefore lies in being able to *predict the future*. This presupposes, amongst other things, a good intelligence service. Realistic predictions are the basis for viable strategic decisions. It is partly a question of creating a picture of changes in the environment through observation, and partly of establishing hypotheses about the future behaviour of the actors (opponents, allies and neutrals).

This takes *knowledge* and *creativity*. Collecting information and intelligence can aid in building up a store of knowledge for strategic considerations. Imagination helps us direct intelligence services and use knowledge in the right way. However, knowledge and creativity are not enough to be able to foretell the future accurately. It also takes *method*. By the same token, method is incredibly important, since it helps us make a complicated situation manageable.

Within the context of strategy, there are in principle three types of theory which can be used in making predictions:

(1) Theories relating to lasting routines.
(2) Theories of rational actors.
(3) Theories of system characteristics.

Lasting routines

This simple theory is always used in making predictions, even if people are not always fully aware of this. The theory says quite simply that what an actor usually does (routine) is probably also what he will do in future. By studying the routines of one's opponents, in other words, one gets an idea of their future actions.

The theory frequently gives good results, but must be applied very carefully: a skilful opponent will be highly aware of the dangers of sticking to routines, and there is therefore a risk that he will break them. The theory must therefore be applied cautiously and complemented by other theories to reduce the risk of being outsmarted.

Rational actors

This theory states that strategic actions are based on rational considerations: in other words, the actors act in the way that is best for them and, if this can be established, their future actions can also be determined. It is therefore useful to observe their actions. This theory can be illustrated using the model presented by lecturers on strategy at the Swedish Military Academy (see reference 8) and shown in Figure 25.

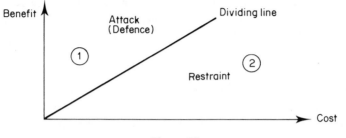

Figure 25

A party considering attack (or defence) will weigh up in rational fashion the costs and benefits of attack (or defence). If the benefits outweigh the costs, the attack (defence) becomes worthwhile, if they do not, then it does not. Position 1 shows such a situation, position 2 the opposite.

One can start from the assumption that all actors are striving for rational behaviour. The problem is simply one of being able to put yourself in your opponent's place and establish what would be rational from his point of view. It can be very helpful to be clear as to what types of actors principally occur (Figure 26).

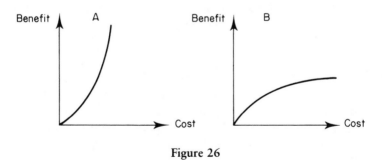

Figure 26

Model A shows an actor acting in a *politically realistic way*. At high levels of cost, there has to be a very good reason for taking action.

Model B, on the other hand, shows someone acting *ideologically*. The higher the stakes, the less the regard for the cost.

It is always important in choosing strategy to be aware what type of opponent one is dealing with. Sweden's actions, for example, are probably governed by a separate concept of rationality from that of Iran's. To foresee one's opponent's reactions and actions realistically, it is therefore important to try and establish his values and standards.

However, reality is more complicated than these simplified models. Firstly, standards probably vary as to whether attack or defence is appropriate. Secondly, a great deal of alternation between realpolitik and ideological action may depend on what scale of costs one is working on. How does the USA's cost/benefit analysis of defending Western Europe in the event of a Soviet attack on Central Europe look, for instance? Something like Figure 27 perhaps.

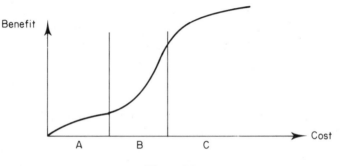

Figure 27

Since the Second World War, the United States has been the guarantor for Western Europe's defence against the Soviets. It has been agreed that any attack on Western Europe is also an attack on the USA. At a low level of costs, one could therefore count on whole-hearted American support. American action in zone A would probably therefore have a strong ideological component: the free world must be given every support in the fight against Communism.

As the cost rises, on the other hand, it is probable that American interest in intervening in the defence of Western Europe would rapidly diminish. In zone B, actions would be distinctly in terms of realpolitik. There can be no sense in starting a devastating nuclear war for relatively limited benefits.

Further up on the scale, in zone C, however, the benefits (stakes) become so considerable that it is probable that American actions would once more take on an ideological character. If it is a question of the entire Western world existing or not—possibly including the

USA—one would have to intervene irrespective of whether this involved nuclear weapons or not.

System characteristics

This theory is also of central importance in all predictions. In any system, there are always some characteristics which mean that in various respects the future will necessarily be shaped in a certain way. If these system characteristics can be established, a vision of the future can be created. The problem is, however, that the situation under discussion is often very complicated and all too often the result is that system characteristics are over-simplified to an inadmissible extent, causing errors to be made.

One example of system characteristics being used far too uncritically at present could be called '*armaments lead to war*'. This theory governs the actions of the peace movement to a large extent; but it has serious faults, as does the opposite theory '*armaments lead to peace*'.

Correctly applied theories of system characteristics are an important aid, however, which we cannot do without. Military strategy is full of such theories which are used in tactical considerations. Systems theories are equally necessary in the marketing war. Theories such as learning curves, BCG models ('Boston Consulting Groups Growth Share Matrix'), and the life-cycle model are major aids, as will be shown later in this book.

All these three theories are of central importance in strategic predictions. They can also be used analogously in assisting us in our analyses. The decision always remains as to what is to be the decisive factor in making strategic decisions. By working methodically, one has a much better chance of success than by trying to hit on a solution in an unstructured fashion.

The important thing is not the present, but the future. *Preparation is more important even than action itself*. It is therefore necessary to have a *good intelligence service and to be able to understand developments*.

9 *Intelligence operations*

Considerations of military strategy are always based on information about the other side. In this chapter, therefore, we will look at intelligence operations in terms of content and method for building up a basis of information. Any military organization maintains a number of intelligence operations on various levels, with whose help qualified intelligence gathering can take place. Collecting information also plays a natural role in the tactical activities of any organization.

Intelligence work

Information is compiled, processed and analysed at staff level, and forms a natural part of operational staff work. Together with information on the strengths and weaknesses of one's own organization, military geography, weather and so on, a base is built up on which strategic assessments can be made. A good intelligence service is therefore vital in planning and carrying out operations. To achieve this, activities must be directed at essentials in good time. Intelligence activities must never be haphazard, but must be methodical and conscious.

These activities are carried out as a continuous circular process with information at the centre rather than as a linear process over time. It can be divided into four functions: direction, collection, processing and furnishing. The process can be illustrated using the so-called 'information cycle' (Figure 28).

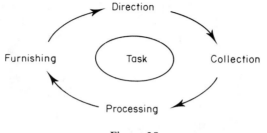

Figure 28

The process uses theories about the future of the kind dealt with in the last chapter. One must always have hypotheses about the actions of the other side: intelligence activities are therefore aimed at monitoring these hypotheses. As long as the results of intelligence agree with the hypotheses, these are valid.

Working out hypotheses on the future actions of the other side is necessary for strategic and tactical action. Hypotheses play a very important role in evaluating the enemy's options (see Chapter 12). This can be shown by the following two examples.

Offensive situation

This can happen if one just 'goes ahead' without having set up an intelligence service (analysing the competition) (Figure 29).

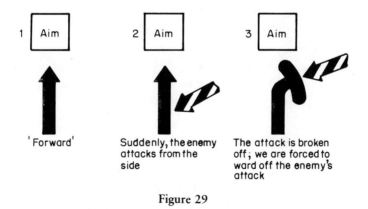

Figure 29

By producing the enemy's options before the attack takes place, that is hypotheses on his actions, we can take suitable decisions in time (Figure 30).

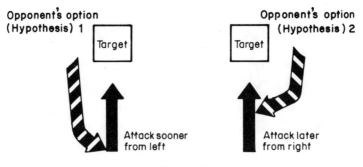

Figure 30

For each of the other side's options, a partial decision can be reached and preparations made to enable it to be carried out rapidly (Figure 31).

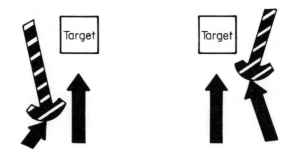

Figure 31

Intelligence services are therefore aimed at establishing *whether* and *when* the other side will attack, and *what alternative* they will choose. In this way, we can act in time and keep the initiative. The chances of reaching the target are therefore large.

Defensive situations

Here we show what can happen if one does not establish an intelligence service but just waits for the enemy's move (Figure 32).

If, on the other hand, we produce various options (hypotheses) before the other side attacks, we can then assess our own options, and then develop one of them as our response. Here, it is useful to start from the *weaknesses* we perceive in the other side, as in Figure 33 for instance.

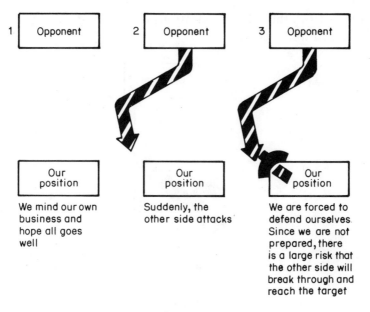

| 1 | Opponent | 2 | Opponent | 3 | Opponent |

| Our position | Our position | Our position |

We mind our own business and hope all goes well

Suddenly, the other side attacks

We are forced to defend ourselves. Since we are not prepared, there is a large risk that the other side will break through and reach the target

Figure 32

One possible decision: our own option on which our decision is based involves an attack on the other side's weak point in option 1. If, instead, the other side attacks 'straight ahead', a partial decision can be made in the context of the main decision which involves our

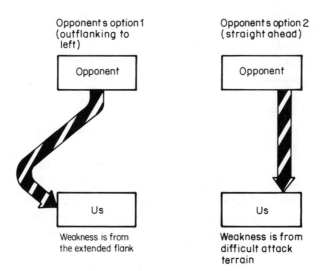

Opponents option 1 (outflanking to left)

Opponent

Us

Weakness is from the extended flank

Opponents option 2 (straight ahead)

Opponent

Us

Weakness is from difficult attack terrain

Figure 33

own attack from the side. Preparations can be made for carrying out the decision rapidly (Figure 34).

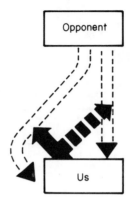

Figure 34

Intelligence activities are then aimed at establishing *if* and *when* the other side will attack and *what options* are open to it. This creates the conditions for being able to act in time. It is very probable that the other side will be forced on to the defensive. Information on the other side therefore plays an important role in strategic analysis. Together with information on the environment and our own strengths and weaknesses, intelligence makes up the basis for strategic planning.

> *When starting to analyse an industry, there is a tendency to go in deep and collect information en masse without any general framework. This error leads in the best case to complication, in the worst case to confusion and waste of resources.* (Michael Porter, *Competitive Strategy*)

The first—and possibly most important—phase of intelligence operations is to set the direction.

First, the so-called 'information requirements' are established. These are guided by our hypotheses as to the other side's actions and the decision and the guidelines which emerged in our deliberations.

Our resources do not allow us to find out *everything* about the other side. We must establish *priorities* as to what we want to gather and concentrate our sources in that direction.

If possible, it may be useful to divide the time span covered by the strategic decision into a number of periods or phases. The aim of this is to ensure that sufficient attention is paid to the dynamics of the situation and changes over the course of time.

A *partial decision* is established for each phase; the information required can then be decided in the light of this:

- to check information hypotheses;
- to ensure that strategic plans are carried out, and to provide the basis for possible partial decisions;
- to take account in good time of any steps by the other side which may affect the carrying out of the strategic decision.

Intelligence activities can generally be formulated in terms of short, simple questions of the kind: What is the other side doing, where, when, how and with what resources?

For example: Is the other side launching its new product as planned previously? Is the launch earlier than expected? Is competitor X managing to break into market X with product Y? Notifying our product to the consumer authorities, environmental authorities? and so on.

Then it is a question of establishing what *sources* and *methods* are available for gathering the information required.

There are two important aspects in developing a strategy for analysing industries and the competition. The first is to define exactly what one is looking for. The second is to define in what order it will be gathered. (Michael Porter, *Competitive Strategy*)

Sometimes, it may happen that information obtained does not fit the hypotheses. If the discrepancy is large, the hypothesis will have to be examined and reformulated. Very often, however, it is more a question of modifying the hypothesis in the light of actual trends.

It has been said that espionage is like putting together a jigsaw puzzle. In the light of what we have said, this is somewhat misleading. Spies should not be left to hunt blindly for pieces of the puzzle, but should be given precise directions in the light of hypotheses and enemy activity (intelligence requirements). As long as the pieces fit together, everything is well and good. If pieces are found that do not fit, however, this means adjusting the board and above all the direction in which intelligence activities are aimed.

It is important to assess the viability of intelligence sources as a basis for evaluating the reliability of information. The reliability of sources varies with their type and level. The further away from the original source, the greater the risk that the facts will be distorted. Note that a clever opponent will also try to mislead us, at least if he sees us as a threat. Differentiate between facts, assumptions and pure hearsay. Only if information is supported by *at least two independent reliable sources* can it be considered as confirmed.

The information gathered is processed, analysed in detail and compiled so as to be able to:

- assess its reliability and certainty;
- check hypotheses and establish future trends;
- provide a basis for strategic considerations in relation to the other side, other parties involved and outside factors.

A good intelligence service is the alpha and omega of strategic action. Good intelligence can give a weaker opponent a real lead over a stronger one. Military organization therefore lays great value on intelligence activities. In business too, their importance is becoming increasingly apparent.

This also means, indirectly, that it is important to protect oneself against enemy intelligence operations. Steps must therefore be taken constantly to:

- conceal one's own situation and forces, activities and intentions;
- mislead enemy intelligence operations;
- combat or disrupt enemy intelligence organizations.

In the Second World War, United States naval intelligence drew its information from the following sources:

- 95 per cent from public official sources;
- 4 per cent from semi-official sources;
- 1 per cent from secret sources.

With processing and analysis, correlation with other information, further information-seeking, persistence, reflection and *imagination*, apparently useless information can be transformed into real 'intelligence'.

JAPANESE INTELLIGENCE OPERATIONS

In the 1950s and 1960s, Japanese engineers were roaming the world in the hunt for state-of-the-art technology for producing motor vehicles, steel, motor cycles, camera, household goods and so on.

These engineers were all-rounders who understood purchasing, production, construction, financing, personnel and marketing questions and were capable of seeing even complex connections between the various functions.

They put a great deal of time and energy into making their journey reports (*Shutcho Hokoku*) as informative and practically applicable as possible. They knew that their colleagues in Japan would be very interested and curious at the well-attended debriefing sessions (*Hokoku-kai*) which would be held when they returned to Japan. They also knew that their reports would be upvalued if they enabled the ideas and technology described in their *Shutcho Hokoku* to be put into practice, which would open the way for them to top positions in their companies.

Kenichi Ohmae, head of McKinsey in Japan, says of a meeting which he had with a Japanese company manager, who was discussing his *Shutcho Hokoku* from the 1960s: 'Back in 1960, I visited this gas turbine plant. The chief engineer proudly spread out every detailed blueprint of their latest product, and explained the unique technological features of the model. So I asked him to give me a copy of the blueprint, but he laughed and said, "You won't need it for a decade". So I went back to the hotel and spent the whole evening recollecting every detail of the design, and by dawn I had the entire turbine reproduced.'

Now the situation in many industries is the other way round. It is we who have to learn from the Japanese. But are we as capable as the Japanese of drawing the lessons from what we see? Are our travellers all-rounders as the Japanese are? Or are they specialists?

And when we make our reports for our audience:

- Are the reports given as much attention as the Japanese *Shutcho Hokoku*?
- Are the de-briefing sessions as well attended, and the questions as detailed?
- Do we get ahead if our reports are marked out, and is it we who become project managers when it comes to putting our ideas into practice?

When Honda and British Leyland (BL) decided to produce a car together in Great Britain, BL sent some engineers to Honda to benefit from Honda's superior production knowledge. This was a failure, amongst other things because none of the BL engineers was an all-rounder, but each was only familiar with a part of the total system. Before BL's personnel had learnt Honda's total system, they had sent more than three hundred foremen and engineers to Japan. According to one of the Honda managers, Honda was forced to spend out 100 times as much as planned for this 'transfer of know-how'.

This example shows how important it is for a company to build up its intelligence organization in a professional way, otherwise the result will be high travelling costs for very little result.

(MAIN SOURCE: *Triad Power*, Kenichi Ohmae, Free Press)

Sources of information

In the marketing war, the following *sources* are available, roughly speaking:

(1) Resources within your own company: the organization as a whole and the different parts. It is incredibly important that people in your own organization recognize the importance of intelligence activities and report information gathered in the course of everyday activities.

(2) *External* sources, such as:
—customers;
—other companies or organizations with which your own is working;
—authorities of various kinds (ministries, patent offices, environmental authorities, local authorities, etc.);
—other companies with some knowledge of the competition;
—people within competing companies;
—political decision-makers and organizations;
—professional or trade organizations, specialist press, house journals;
—journalists, newspapers and magazines, radio and TV;
—annual reports, lectures, product catalogues;
—conferences, trade fairs and exhibitions;
—consultants;
—various databanks: a large number of databases are now accessible via host organizations. Examples of these are Dialog (USA), Data Star (Switzerland), Infoline (UK) and ESA-Quest (Italy).

Some of the databases that can be used for business information are Arthur D. Little/Online, Management Contents, ABI/Inform, Predicast, Textline, Nexis etc.

Different sources yield different types of information. Sources may be easier or more difficult to access and more or less reliable.

Let us look more closely at the main sources, beginning with the most readily available:

Read what competitors write about themselves

ANNUAL REPORTS, where they exist in detailed form, are a valuable source of information. It is best if you can study and compare reports for a number of consecutive years (say five). The managing director's report in particular can say a great deal. This is normally aimed at a number of categories simultaneously: shareholders, employees, customers and sometimes also competitors. Descriptions of proposed technological development in the company, for example, *may* be made with the idea of keeping competitors in their place; or it may be a real disclosure which the MD is making to give employees and shareholders positive information.

Annual reports on subsidiaries should be viewed critically. These companies' reports are mainly produced for the parent company and its evaluation. The results may therefore be misleading.

HOUSE JOURNALS vary widely in quality and the attention they pay to facts which should not be let out. But if, in analysing the competition, you want to go into depth, house journals may say a great deal about a company's fighting spirit.

PRODUCT CATALOGUES are designed for customers and sometimes even partly for competitors. Anyone familiar with the products may find something of interest in studying changes from one edition to the next: what quality could obviously not be achieved in price or production terms, what direction are the competition going in? and so on.

PRODUCT ADS. A company's success depends on its products. The way in which they are presented may say a great deal about the company's long-term strategy.

EMPLOYMENT ADS are often a useful source. What skills are being looked for, and how are the desired qualifications described and, perhaps most important but most difficult for the investigator: who got the job, i.e. how far did the qualifications required agreed with what they were satisfied with?

Annual reports, house journals, product catalogues, product and job advertisements give a clear idea of the values guiding an organization. They are therefore of prime importance in analysing the competition.

ARTICLES in technical and economic journals *may* give useful information, but frequently do not. Companies with an active information service limit and clean articles quite well. There are technical experts, however, who write for their colleagues in other companies and economists who love to talk about how and why they have developed the world's best commercial control system and so on.

INTERVIEWS in the press and on TV are easy to get hold of but vary widely in quality. Often they are far too general, but sometimes of course they may be a hit, particularly for those who know the company well from other sources.

Take advantage of what others know about the competition

CUSTOMERS of course have a lot to say about competitors, such as how efficient they are. (It is remarkable that, in spite of this, customers continue to buy our products!) Joking apart, customer's views are valuable. They may help in clarifying which competitors are most dangerous and why. When all distortion factors have been evaluated, the total can say a great deal.

SUPPLIERS are used to being asked about competitors, and they have a great deal to say which they will, on the natural condition that nothing is passed on. This is natural, since they have a number of loyalties to balance.

COMPETITORS themselves can also be an excellent source of information, if used with a little finesse. You can talk about markets where you are not in competition or general conditions important for common activities. And in particular about other competitors. Handled correctly, a 'them and us' situation soon arises. This is in fact a common reaction with many people. There are ethical limits. Discussions of this kind may be made with all one's cards on the table, however. We do not claim to be anything other than what we are, that is a competitor wanting to know as much as possible about others in the same market. It is often a question here of buying information with information, and of course the information we give must be completely true. But we can choose what we let out.

YOUR OWN SALESFORCE also has information to give. You should not be surprised if parts of this information resemble information received from customers. A salesforce gets a great deal of its knowledge of the market from them. In assessing information, you should also remember that the customer's tendency to over-value the competition will be reinforced by the salesman. Salespeople like to think that their company's products and prices are worse than those of the competition. 'I don't know how they expect us to sell this rubbish—but we do!' Providing you are aware of this risk of distortion, salespeople can be an excellent source of information.

70

Salespeople are also very important when it comes to gathering operational intelligence on competitors. They should therefore be trained in competitive analysis and involved in sales and marketing planning. The chance of being involved in a company's business ideas, strategy and culture is important for fighting morale. The company's inner strength creates opportunities for good intelligence gathering at this level. It can sometimes be worthwhile *working with competitors* to collect good information. This applies mainly in the field of product development, where a weaker party wants to build up its fighting potential, as shown in the following example taken from the book *Car Wars* by Robert Sobel.

THE JAPANESE CAR INDUSTRY

In the 1950s, the Japanese car industry was way behind the European and American industries, and they had no way of getting the research and development resources needed to catch up.

What they did was to obtain licences. They also copied or 'borrowed' from their Western competitors. But this wasn't enough: to catch up, they had to work with Western car manufacturers to attain their technological superiority.

In 1952, *Nissan* signed a contract with Austin to produce 1200 light goods vehicles in Japan over a five-year period.

Izuzu had a similar contract with Rootes to produce Hillman goods vehicles in Japan.

Hino had a contract with Renault to produce 1300 Renault cars.

Mitsubishi worked with the American Jeep to produce jeeps for the Japanese market.

These co-operation projects were short-lived, and lasted only for as long as it took the Japanese to learn what they wanted about their European and American competitors.

This example is intended to show how working with competitors can be used for 'transfer of know-how', at the same time as we promise cooperation with competitors ahead of us to gather the information we need.

Working with competitors is often necessary to reinforce our fighting potential on the market, but care should also be taken to ensure that the competitors' aim is not to gather information as well.

There are many *methods of information gathering*, of which the most important are:

- *Reconnaissance*: for example, visits to competing companies and their branches, sales drives, etc. Visits to trade fairs and exhibitions. Observation of competitors' activities in the field, etc.
- *Questioning*: customers, suppliers, your own salesforce, other employees who know something about the competition, distributors, dealers, job applicants working for competitors, employees and former employees of competitors, consultants, etc.
- *Studying literature*: annual reports, product catalogues, product advertisements, journal articles, press articles, interviews on radio, TV, applications for concessions, inquiries, credit information, etc.
- *Materials analysis*: e.g. of competitors' products.
- *Cooperation*: with friendly companies/organizations.
- *Working with competitors*: for a limited period.
- *Taking on competitors' key personnel.*

The last method is very useful and need not be unethical or lead to a deterioration in relationships with competitors if handled with finesse.

In 1984, Chrysler launched its T115 Minivan (practically a lorry in miniature) on the US market, which was immediately a great sales success.

Lee Iacocca, who took over at Chrysler in 1978 and who saved the company from its major crisis in 1979–81, becoming a national hero into the bargain, was often asked in his lectures to students of economics, 'How could you as a businessman put down seven hundred million dollars on the line three years in advance while you were going broke?' In his book, *Iacocca*, he gives the answer: 'The minivan was actually born over at Ford!'

THE CHRYSLER MINIVAN

In 1974, Hal Sperlich and Lee Iacocca (at that time MD at Ford) were working on a project known as Mini-Max. This was a front-wheel-drive van, roomy inside but small externally. $500,000 was put into a market survey, which came up with three important requirements:

(1) Mini-Max must be comfortable to get into and out of, even for women in skirts or dresses.
(2) The vehicle's height must enable it to fit into a standard garage.
(3) It should be fitted with a deformation zone of some decimetres to give reasonable protection in the event of an accident.

If Ford took sufficient account of these three main requirements in its development work, it could look forward to a market potential of 800,000 vehicles in 1974, according to the market survey.

In his book, Iacocca describes what happened when he presented the project to Henry Ford II.

'Forget it,' said Henry. 'I don't want to experiment.' 'Experiment?' I said. 'The Mustang was an experiment. The Mark III was an experiment. This car is not an experiment. It is another winner.' But Henry didn't buy it.

So, instead of producing the Mini-Max at Ford, Sperlich and Iacocca did it at Chrysler in 1984. 'And now it's Ford's customers we are stealing,' says Iacocca with ill-concealed glee.

In his book, Iacocca also says that when it became apparent to him that Henry Ford II was manoeuvring to get rid of him, he took a number of steps to improve his future freedom to manoeuvre.

Some months before the end, Iacocca asked Ford's finance head J. Edward Lundy to draw up a list of Ford's best finance people. Outwardly a routine question, but . . .

When Iacocca was fired and then after some weeks began to work as boss at Chrysler, the list came in useful. Iacocca looked through the list and then took on Gerald Greenwald as Chrysler's head of finance—the best of the candidates on the list. After a few months at Chrysler, Iacocca had filled almost all the top positions with former Ford employees.

This example is intended to show how dangerous it can be for a company's key personnel to be 'picked up' by a competitor; in fact, it shows only a part of what can happen.

(SOURCE: *Iacocca*, Lee Iacocca, Bantam Books)

Materials analysis was mentioned in our list as a method of collecting important information on competitors and their products. Since this method is both common and important, we will deal with some further viewpoints here. The method consists of getting hold of a competitor's product, taking it apart and analysing its parts in terms of function, material and manufacturing methods.

In his book, *The Mind of the Strategist* (McGraw-Hill Book Company, New York, 1982), Kenichi Ohmae describes the technique in great detail. He points out that materials analysis of competitors' products is now routine in Japan. In practice, all manufacturing companies use it to keep an eye on the competition and to compare their products with similar ones.

The analysis is in two parts: analysis of the product's quality and reliability (VE—Value Engineering), and of the price in relation to assumed production costs (VA—Value Analysis). Together, these give an idea of the product's competitiveness and give ideas as to how we can improve our competitiveness.

Intelligence operations must be organized in the light of requirements

The need to analyse requirements and organize intelligence operations in the light of these becomes particularly important when studying companies involved in a number of different markets and customer categories—'diversified' companies.

Their business must first be divided into SBUs—Strategic Business Units such as

- selling a specific group of products or services;
- to a specific group of customers;
- in competition with a specific group of competitors.

SBUs are the basis for business planning, both short- and long-term. These are units which compete with one another—not the company, which may consist of more than one SBU. Almost personal SBUs can sometimes have such central support from the company that the competitive situation is distorted. This can be one of the most difficult questions in the analysis.

Division into *MARKETS* is the next step. Conditions for intelligence operations can vary dramatically from one market to the next.

SEGMENTATION of the individual markets—that is division of markets by groups of customers with similar requirements—gives a final division of the competitive situation in meaningful terms.

Some competitors may of course be in competition with more than one SBU or be in markets serving more than one category of customer. This should in such cases emerge very clearly. Frequently, however, analysis succeeds in giving a simple, systematic division of competing forces so that a clear main competitor can be defined for each market segment. This is then useful in formulating information requirements and directing intelligence operations.

74

Communications and follow-up

The result of intelligence services must not be allowed to languish in some filing cabinet without any actual effect on operations. For it to give the intended result, it must be communicated quickly, clearly and relevantly to those affected.

Communication within your own company should be ordered and, if so required, in a particular order. Other companies and organizations with whom you are cooperating may also be involved if necessary.

Sometimes, certain sources themselves should be given the overall assessment. This gives them feedback and an overall picture which aids further information-gathering.

At the same time, it is important for competitors not to hear our most important assessments of them. Communications must therefore be discerning. Evaluations of competitors' options always have a high confidential value.

Information collected and processed provides the basis for new assessments of competitors, markets, customer requirements and so on.

A new assessment is *compared* with the previous assessment which was the basis for current strategic decisions. The results of the comparison are sent to decision-makers, management groups and so on. If there are *major differences*, the result may be a new decision or decisions. If the differences are small, there may be smaller changes within the overall decision or execution of a prepared partial strategy and some changes in the direction of intelligence operations.

> *Know the enemy and know yourself; in a hundred battles you will never be in peril. When you are ignorant of the enemy but know yourself, your chances of winning or losing are equal. If ignorant of both your enemy and of yourself, you are certain in every battle to be in peril.* (Sun Tzu, 500 BC)

Security operations

Security and intelligence operations are closely connected with one another, and should therefore be allocated to the same unit or department in a company. The aim of security services is to protect your own company or organization from competitors' *intelligence activities* and other activities threatening security (e.g. disinformation, rumours, etc.). To prevent competitors buying information from employees within your own company or acquiring your key personnel, it is important to work closely with personnel functions.

What we looked at earlier gives a good idea of what a company has to protect itself against in terms of competitors' lawful intelligence operations. We have not looked at unlawful methods; but we must be fully aware that it is not certain that the competition will have the same ethical standards as we do. Unlawful intelligence activities exist, and we can be prepared for them. Security must therefore cover this area as well. Theft and regular industrial espionage are a fact of life. We must be on our guard and protect ourselves against both lawful and unlawful intelligence activities.

To be able to protect your company, you must first *establish* hypotheses on activities threatening its security and direct parts of your intelligence operations against them.

10 Strategies for the marketing war

We will now go on and apply military strategy more tangibly to modern marketing warfare. We will present five attack and six defence strategies which together cover the entire field of conceivable strategies.

Before we do this, however, we must once more emphasize two important factors which must always be established, irrespective of the situation. The first concerns the *fighting potential* on the basis of which one is acting and the possibilities of improving this through cooperation with competitors. The second relates to the importance of creating the maximum *freedom of action* before the offensive.

Working with competitors

To create a position of strength or fighting potential, it may often be very worthwhile working together with one or more competitors in the short- or long-term.

MATSUSHITA

With the brand names JVC, Panasonic, Technics and Quasar, the Matsushita group has a 15 per cent share in the US for video equipment under its own brand names. In fact, its share of the market is 45 per cent more than that, since the company is a so-called 'original equipment manufacturer' (OEM) or supplier to such companies as RCA, Magnavox, General Electric, Sylvania and Montgomery Ward.

In Europe, Matsushita's own sales give it a 33 per cent share of the market. As OEM supplier to EMI and Thorn in Great Britain, Telefunken and SABA in Germany, Thomson CSF in France and Granada in Spain, however, it has a further 35 per cent of the market.

This means that the Matsushita group's share in the video equipment market is some 60 per cent in the USA and 70 per cent in Europe, while it is also the market leader in Japan. In other words, Matsushita has achieved a crushing superiority over the competition. By working together with various competitors in the distribution sector, it can increase its purchasing and production volume and the number of units over which to distribute Research and Development costs on.

(SOURCE: *Triad Power*, Kenichi Ohmae, Free Press)

VOLVO BM

In 1984, VOLVO BM and the American CLARK EQUIPMENT company, Michigan, decided to work together in many respects. The background was that VOLVO BM was the leader in the European market for various types of construction machinery (centrally-steered dumpers, etc.) but was weak where other types of machines were concerned. VOLVO BM was poorly represented on the American market. CLARK's position was basically the opposite. VOLVO BM continued to sell its machines successfully in the Middle East, but had difficulty breaking into the South American market. CLARK, on the other hand, was strong in Brazil.

Through working together with CLARK, VOLVO BM has access to CLARK's nationwide distribution network in the US and Brazil for distributing those types of machinery where it has a very competitive product and CLARK does not. The reverse applies for CLARK in the European and Middle East markets.

In spite of this cooperation, both Caterpillar and Komatsu are bigger overall, which is a tough challenge for VOLVO BM–CLARK.

Product development costs, which are rapidly rising the whole world over, make it necessary to share out development work to reduce development costs per unit of sales. The phenomenon of the unit costs dropping by 20–30 per cent per doubling of accumulated volume is called the 'learning curve'.

This is due not only to *advantages of scale* but also to:

- the learning effect;
- changes in construction, materials and production;
- technological developments.

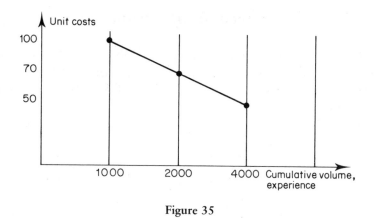

Figure 35

There are four reasons in all for the experience effect:

- *Learning*: personal, group, cooperation, etc.
- *Economies of scale*: large purchase volume, larger manufacturing volume, and Research and Development costs can be spread over a larger volume (larger denominators in division).
- *Construction, etc.*: over the course of time, and as the number of units produced increases, construction improves, production methods develop, cheaper materials are used, etc.
- *Technology*: increased use of technology such as mechanization robots, more computers and communications aids, more electronics in production, possible change of technology.

The effect of the learning curve on product development, purchasing and distribution is therefore a reason for cooperation. 'Small is not beautiful', at least in this case.

You don't need a calculator to see that if GM's expenses on a particular item were $1 million and they sold a hundred thousand cars, each buyer paid an additional $10. And if Chrysler's costs were the same, but we had only twenty thousand buyers, each one would pay an additional $50.

But that's only research and development. Then we have to manufacture the stuff. Here the same disproportion applies, except with larger numbers. GM, with its huge sales volume, can build them cheaper and sell them cheaper than we can. And so the gap widens. (Lee Iacocca, head of Chrysler)

Freedom of action

Irrespective of which strategy is chosen, the aim is to create the maximum freedom of action by preventing one's opponent from increasing his share of the market or, if possible, deterring him from entering the market at all.

Freedom of action is created by *lateral manoeuvring* chosen well in view of the level of conflict. It can be created by such methods as

- Working in industrial associations or standardization committees to set the rules as favourably as possible for one's own goods and services and unfavourably to those of competitors.
- Getting politicians and journalists to see that we should be able to export freely, while engaging at the same time in the fight against 'unjustified' dumping on our domestic markets.
- By involving oneself widely in political-economic debates and presenting the view of business on everything from wage agreements to child care.

Freedom of action can also be improved by *direct manoeuvring* on and around the battlefield. As we have already pointed out, it is important to create a good starting position so that one can use the advantages of the terrain in the coming battles. As far as attack is concerned, this means holding an adequate position from which to attack and engaging in conflict on favourable ground. In defence, it is likewise important to hold key ground and collect one's forces on easily-defended positions.

Freedom of action can be improved with the aid of feint operations with the aim of simply confusing the other side. It is often enough, for example, to precede the main attack by a feint attack in a secondary direction to make the other side concentrate its defences in the 'wrong' sector.

Always remember the most important thing: formulate an aim, and ensure that *all* actions work together towards that aim.

Attacking strategies

We will now look at the various attacking strategies. The greatest effect will probably be achieved by combining some of the five strategies presented here as circumstances dictate. They can also be combined with defensive strategies.

1. Frontal attack

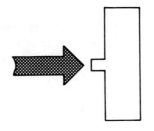

Attack competitors' strengths instead of their weaknesses! This strategy is completely in line with classic direct strategy. To succeed, the attacker needs real superiority of forces in the form of a better product, significantly lower cost levels, greater sales force, greater financial resources and so on. Companies which work hard on product and process development, 'just in time' production/ purchasing, materials development and which have a large volume to distribute are using the logic of the learning curve and can therefore always offer the same product at a lower price or a better product at the same price. They work in the logic of the virtuous circle (Figure 36).

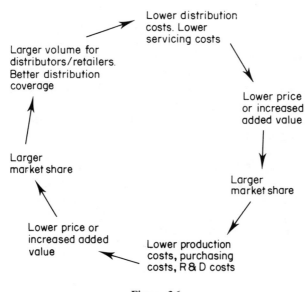

Figure 36

81

IBM

Gene Amdahl, who had been one of the main architects of IBM's successful 360 series, wanted to build an advanced mainframe computer using LSI (large-scale integration) technology. IBM said no. So Amdahl left, and got the backing of the Heizer Corporation, Nixdorf and Fujitsu.

Amdahl's strategy was simple: by using existing LSI technology which was superior to the hybrid circuits of the 360 series, he would build computers smaller, cheaper, faster and with more capacity. Not only that, but they would be a good deal cheaper than the 360 series for customers who did not need IBM's large service organization. There was no need for him to create any software, since all the computers could use IBM's (IBM compatibility).

Amdahl's first machine, the 470/V6, introduced in 1975, was sold to such customers as Hughes Aircraft, General Motors, NASA and AT & T. By the spring, he had supplied over 50 computers to very pleased customers. Amdahl's attack on IBM was followed by Control Data, National Semiconductor, Burroughs, NCR, UNIVAC and a half-dozen new companies.

IBM's counter-attack began by its salesmen warning customers what would happen to their servicing if Amdahl or National Semiconductor pulled out of the market. They also raised the possibility that IBM's service and maintenance on circuitry in Amdahl's computers would be reduced or cease altogether. This was a minor taste of what was to come.

In March 1977, IBM introduced the 3033 series, with twice the capacity of the 360/168 at two-thirds the price. Their competitors took fright; but not Amdahl.

Three days later, Amdahl announced the introduction of two new computers: the 470 V/5, cheaper than IBM's 370/168, and the 470 V/7, giving more value for capacity than IBM's 3033.

IBM now realized that the frontal attack had failed, and went over to a strategy of attrition, by putting significantly more resources into development than Amdahl or anyone else could provide. The strategy now was slowly to strip away Amdahl's financial resources. With the aid of the introduction of the 303X, the 4300 and later the H series, the seal was finally set on Amdahl's ruin.

The psychological hold IBM then created over its competitors by showing them that they could go further than anyone when it came to price-cutting if it came to direct competition has left a deep impression on the industry.

Who dares to challange fortress IBM?

(SOURCE: *IBM in Transition*, Robert Sobel, Times Books)

JAPANESE COMPANIES

Japanese companies which are well established in given markets literally crush their competitors by using price levels below those of the competition in real terms. In combination with high quality and high technology, this gives a fruitful competitive force.

Canon's victorious drive throughout the world, first in calculators but later in cameras, typewriters and smaller copiers, is a combination of high levels of technology, neat design, low production costs thanks to well-thought-out designs and high volume. Who can beat the Japanese in the typical mass-production industry?

OK
(The consumer-owned oil company)

In 1984, OK scrapped all the petrol price reductions which were flourishing in Sweden and intended, as it said, to give all its members a 12 ore discount so as to favour its regular customers. By going on to the frontal attack in this way against some of the biggest oil companies in the world, they launched a war of attrition which they could only lose. OK was forced as a result to announce in whole-page advertisements to state that the discount applied to everybody. In practice, the result was a price reduction of 12 ore.

What did OK do wrong? OK had not analysed the strength and probable reaction of its competitors. It is not enough to be the biggest in Sweden if Exxon, Kuwait Petroleum (Gulf) and Shell are the competition. 'Know your enemy.'

One year later, OK reported a loss of 400 million kronor for 1984. 'Senseless petrol war on the Swedish market, the sky-high dollar exchange rate and large-scale investment in (as it turned out) unprofitable refineries effectively contributed to the loss,' said OK chief Lennart Andersson.

Some weeks later, energy minister Birgitta Dahl began to make rumbling noises in the press about unjustified price-cutting by the multinational oil companies on the Swedish market (lateral manoeuvring) and said that she was considering intervening. Those who know their history, however, will not be deceived so easily, but know that OK started the 'senseless petrol war', to quote Lennart Andersson, head of OK.

2. Flanking attack

An opponent's weakest points are very often the flank and rear. A flanking attack is therefore aimed at *an opponent's weakness* rather than his strengths.

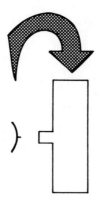

The attack is carried out by concentrating one's forces against the opponent's weak points or geographical areas where he is poorly represented. This can also be expressed as follows, which is more creative and has a much greater potential: work on customer needs which the competition does not notice or worry about.

> *If you're Ford, you've got to beat GM to the punch. You've got to find market niches that they haven't even thought of. You can't go head to head with them—they're just too big. You've got to outflank them.*
> (Chrysler chief Lee Iacocca)

PHARMACIA

In certain eye operations, such as those for cataracts, you have to open up the anterior chamber of the eye. This is full of fluid, the so-called aqueous humour. If the fluid escapes, the chamber collapses and operating can become difficult.

This is where hyaluronate is used, which is obtained from coxcombs. The Swedish pharmaceutical company Pharmacia markets this in the preparation Healon. Hyaluronate is an incredibly viscous, sluggish mass which can hold the anterior chamber apart during the operation and for some days afterwards, until new natural aqueous humour is created. The medium also forms a protective layer during operations so that sensitive parts of the eye such as the cornea are not damaged.

Through its process expertise (the separation products division within Pharmacia), high-price strategy, unconventional sales approach (famous surgeons lecturing on the excellence of Healon at congresses of eye surgeons) and through the preparation being registered as a surgical aid instead of a medical aid (3 months for approval in the USA), Pharmacia has created an extremely profitable introduction card to the field of eye surgery (opthalmology).

ACO

When ACO, which is owned by the state chemists, wanted to introduce its new skin-care series, they made a precise study of the competition's products, marketing and distribution channels. Then they went over to a massive attack against their weaknesses. In other words, a typical flank attack.

The traditional way of selling skin-care products looks like this:

(1) *Products*: Often unnecessarily complicated, containing far too many ingredients without any main effect but with increased risk of allergic reaction as a result.
ACO's concept: Simple, well-tested principles, based on medical knowledge.

(2) *Consumer market segment*: Low awareness, poor education.
ACO: Aware, well-educated.

(3) *Perfume*: Strong, distinctive.
ACO: Not so strong, neutral, unperfumed.

(4) *Contents*: Kept secret 'to create an air of mystery'.
ACO: Openly declared and stated.

(5) *Packaging*: Fancy design. Gold, silver. Sometimes low on technical quality.
ACO: Simple design. High technical quality.

(6) *Advertising message*: Emotionally oriented.
ACO: Product-oriented.

(7) *Choice of media*: Weekly press (company's message depending on editorial environment).
ACO: Daily press, even evening papers.

(8) *Price*: High (high prices can generate an image of high quality).
ACO: Low.

(9) *Emphasis in marketing mix*: Personal sales to distributors and consumers (via cosmetologists).
ACO: Communication via mass media.

(10) *Distribution*: Selective mercantile level (beauty parlours, boutiques, department stores).
ACO: Selective technical milieu (mainly via chemists).

What ACO did was thus precisely the opposite of the traditional concept of the industry.

Comparative advertising (guerrilla attack) gave the competition some shocks. Advertisements were aimed at well-known brands (main competitors) and under each package was the price per kg. ACO is of course the

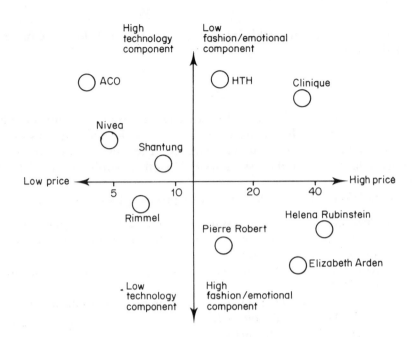

Figure 37. Positional analysis—cosmetics market
SOURCE: *ACO Skin-care: a Practical Case*, Göran Alsterlind, ACO International.

cheapest skin-care brand. The text read: 'Do you think your skin will notice the difference' (between 62 kronor/kilo and 240 kronor/kilo)?

VOLKSWAGEN

British, French and Italian car companies had failed to gain a foothold in the American market, in spite of the fact that many Americans were favourably disposed towards small European cars. The main reason for this failure was poor product quality, but above all inadequate servicing and spares organization.

American small car owners might have to wait a month for spares from Europe; and when they *did* finally arrive, there was no guarantee that they would fit, which would mean that the customer might have to wait another few weeks.

Under its dynamic MD, Heinz Nordhoff, Volkswagen, which metaphorically and literally pulled itself out of the ashes after the Second World War, aimed right from the start at producing a high-quality economy car.

Although the markets were crying out for the VW 'beetle', with long

86

delivery times as a result, VW frequently stopped production—sometimes for weeks—if quality did not reach Nordhoff's standards.

Heinz Nordhoff was probably the first in the industry to insist so obstinately on product quality. Like Henry Ford with his 'model T', Nordhoff refused to make changes in his model, and the basic concept of the 'beetle' remained largely intact until it was dropped at the end of the 1970s.

In the late 1940s and early 1950s, VW rapidly gained popularity in Europe, especially with the many American soldiers in West Germany. When VW later decided to break into the American market, Nordhoff sent Will van den Kamp over to head the operation. Kamp was a perfectionist, and chose only dealers who were prepared to give their whole effort to VW. Above all, dealers had to be prepared to keep proper spares stocks and use dedicated, well-trained mechanics—VW specialists.

VW quickly built up a good reputation for its excellent service, just as it had done for economy and product quality. Its recipe for success on the American market was as follows:

—To establish itself on the market with a very economical to run but high-quality small car, at a very competitive selling price.
—An exceptional service and spares organization which was the admiration of its competitors.
—Taking advantage of young Americans' need to rebel against authority—in this case, against their elders' taste in cars. Driving around in a VW was economical and thrifty, in contrast to the giant American 'gas-guzzlers'.
—To foment the VW myth, which claimed that VW had made the perfect, timeless car, although common sense should have told car buyers otherwise, that with all the reports on the VW's poor stability in side winds, carbon monoxide poisoning, fires after crashes—to name only a few of the 'beetle''s disadvantages.

In 1970, VW sold 569,000 'beetles', but then the slide began, due to the VW's outdated basic design and changes in consumer tastes, and it was then that the Japanese car invasion began to get under way.

In 1969, the Japanese sold 260,000 cars in the US; two years later, the figure was 703,000.

(MAIN SOURCE: *Car Wars*, Robert Sobel, Truman Talley)

TOYOTA

Toyota prepared its entry into the US market very carefully. The company knew that the small-car segment was where it could outdo the competition. This segment is dominated by Volkswagen, who Toyota saw as their main opponent.

By asking Volkswagen owners what they thought were the good and bad points in their cars, they found out what the product features were that a small car should have to win customers from VW. Then Toyota built the 'ideal' small car, priced it lower than the VW, put out much more advertising and gave dealers generous margins. Toyota set its sights on the weakest segment in the US market (small cars), saw VW the market leaders as its main opponent and offered VW owners (but also other small-car owners) more value for their money.

(SOURCE: Kotler-Fahey, 'The world champion marketers: the Japanese', *Journal of Business Strategy*, Summer 1982)

SPENDRUP
(The small Swedish brewery)

Spendrups had got the Lowenbrau agency and used this as their entry card to government alcohol shops* and restaurants. In spite of this, they were only one fourteenth the size of Pripps, the largest Swedish brewery (state-owned).

Pripps had failed to give discerning beer drinkers a good beer. The Grangesberg brewery saw its opportunity here, and took it: they changed to a Danish name (the owners were called Spendrup), created a full-bodied class II beer which tasted like strong beer, gave it an exclusive packaging, and exclusive and step-by-step launching and high-price strategy to underline its high quality.

The elegant popular beer was first sold at Stockholm's most famous restaurant the Operakällaren, then at 10 luxury restaurants in Stockholm, then in restaurants all over Sweden and finally in grocery stores in Dalarna and so on. For consumers, it is just this class II beer which is the most obvious symbol of the company's success.

It should be realized that Lowenbrau as a 'star product' was a precondition, both technically and in market and distribution terms, for Spendrup's success. There was no reason for Spendrup's step-by-step introduction at production capacity before resources could be reallocated.

The situation can be clarified by using a competitive profile analysis.

* State monopoly shops for sales of spirits, wine and strong beers.

The situation before the flank attack

Market: beer market
Geographical area: Sweden
Geographical area: Sweden
Competitor: Pripps

Market success factors   Position relative to competitor

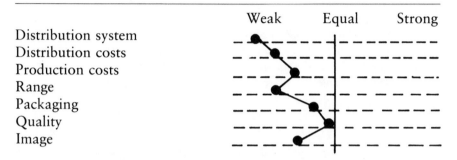

Competitive profile analysis clarifying flank attack

Market: premium beer market
Geographical area: Stockholm restaurants
Competitor: Pripps

Market success factors   Position relative to competitor

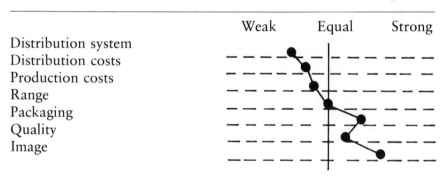

By putting as least as much effort as Pripps into a limited market segment, David was able to slay Goliath. A not inconsiderable part of Spendrup's success was due to the fact that Pripps had nodded off in its market dominance.

HONDA

In 1950, *Honda* had only 200 dealers. The company wrote a letter to 18,000 cycle dealers in Japan and offered to teach people how to sell and repair Honda motorcycles. In one swoop, they picked up 5000 new dealers. In the US, Honda opened the dormant pleasure market with slogans such as 'You meet the nicest people on a Honda'. What Honda was doing was changing the image of the motorcycle, and in this way it succeeded in doubling the size of the motorcycle market in the USA.

Honda's taking the position of world leader for motorcycles is a textbook example of 'gradual action', that is, the artichoke strategy. You concentrate your resources on a few products (125 cc, 250 cc) and take a geographic market. Climb. Then take the next market. Climb. Introduce more products (350 cc, 450 cc). Take another market, and so on.

PHARMACIA—DRUGS

Extract from Pharmacia's Swedish annual report, 1983:

Company direction:
The division develops, produces and markets drugs and associated products for treatment of illnesses. Great emphasis is laid on developing products which treat causes and not just symptoms.

The strategic programme for the 1980s involves a new direction towards *substances naturally occurring in the human body, biomolecules, and biomechanic mechanisms*. This strategic reorientation has been completed and has proved very successful.

A large number of research projects have grown from this and led to a vital research portfolio with a good balance between short- and long-term projects. The interest shown by the rest of the world in Pharmacia's new research orientation and the strategic emphasis on direct customer contact have resulted in a series of proposed projects and product offers from outsiders.

Pharmacia's pharmaceutical division has in this way reached an international leading position in work on what are called '*tomorrow's pharmaceuticals*' which represent the biomedical branch within the international pharmaceutical industry.

Research:
The flow of new research projects has been very strong since the division's strategic reorientation in 1980. Its research capacity has also been extended greatly as a result.

Between 1980 and 1983, the division's research budget grew almost five times over. In 1983 alone, input grew by 55 per cent. The pharmaceutical division's costs of research and development accounted for 11 per cent of turnover in 1983 as against 5.5 per cent in 1980, and will continue to grow further in 1984.

The orientation of research towards products with biological specificity means amongst other things that the number of interesting projects has grown very rapidly. The idea of biomedical research can be compared to a clutch of ants' eggs, while conventional pharmaceutical industry concentrates on a single ostrich egg. The probability of success for a project is therefore equally great for each unit, no matter what the size.

As the reader can see, the flank attack using intelligence, or rather creativity, wins over raw strength (frontal attack).

In military language, 'Change the battlefield', if it does not fit. Do not fight in the open against a materially stronger opponent, but on ground which is better suited to your resources.

Or fight with superior technology. Israel's knocking out the Syrian air warning system and aeroplanes during the Lebanon war is an example of electronic warfare on a large scale. Biotechnology, fibre optics, composite materials and the whole electronics revolution give the same opportunities for devastating superiority over the competition.

JAPANESE TV COMPANIES

The first oil price shock in 1973 led to enormous increases in costs of power and other raw materials and an increased rate of inflation which pushed up international wage levels.

Japan adapted faster than any other country to the consequences, however. The Japanese government embarked on a restrictive wage and financial policy to keep down inflation and speeded up construction of nuclear power stations to reduce the dependency on expensive oil (lateral manoeuvres).

Japanese colour TV companies changed their manufacturing technology. They threw out transistors and replaced them with integrated circuits, which enabled them to produce TV sets with only half the number of components of those of their European and American competitors. At the same time, they replaced the long lines of power-heavy fitters with semi-automatic production lines.

The result of all these efforts was colour TVs of higher quality at only half the price of the competition in Europe and the States.

The competitors, who realized that they were on the way to being completely 'massacred' by the total superiority of the Japanese, were forced to use 'lateral manoeuvring' to make their governments set up various kinds of import restrictions against the Japanese export offensive. By giving themselves a few years breathing-space and through large-scale investment, they then caught up with the Japanese.

(SOURCE: *Triad Power*, Kenichi Ohmae, Free Press)

3. Encirclement (surrounding and attrition)

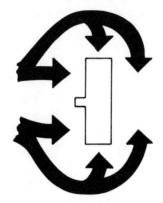

If you are above all financially stronger than your competitors and do not have the ability to reach a decisive conclusion quickly, surrounding may be the right strategy. This strategy involves attacking the competition in their main sectors, weak sectors, new sectors, subcontractors and distribution systems. By fighting on all fronts, you can win—but with limited effort on each front.

In this way, you can force your competitors to split their resources, which exposes any weaknesses on their part in terms of markets and product areas. This enables rapid incursions and forces competitors to make a strategic retreat.

Figure 38 shows what very frequently happens when a new product is introduced on the market.

(SOURCE: Gunnar Dahlsten)

Gunnar Dahlsten (director and former managing director of Mölnlycke and Swedish Match) tends in his excellent lectures to emphasize that in fact the picture is far too positive.

This means that it takes over 3.5 years before the cumulative result, and 4.5 years before the accumulated liquidity is positive after a new product is introduced on the market.

The alert reader will already have realized how to use the situation. If you are stronger financially, by introducing products at a fast rate

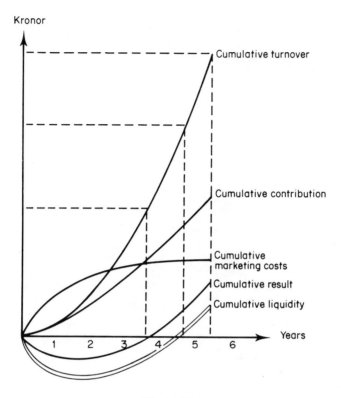

Figure 38

and in a number of markets you can force competitors to follow into a liquidity-straining field. This weakens their position further, which increases the relative competitiveness of the stronger company (fighting potential) and hence also its negotiating strength and freedom of action.

The financially weaker company must avoid being drawn into such a war of attrition at any price. The competition and rules of the game must be altered so that the balance of strength is more equal. The key concept here is cooperation with competitors and the aim is to reduce marketing costs.

Companies can do this, for example, by joint marketing efforts with one or more competitors. Or they can have their products marketed via a number of distribution channels and possibly under another name, that is become so-called 'Original Equipment Manufacturers' (OEMs). They can have their product included as part of a larger package or market the products of their main competitor's worst international enemy—with proper financial backing, of course, so that the aim of reducing marketing costs is achieved. The idea of cooperation applies of course to most company functions.

Conclusion: Work with competitors, sub-contractors and distributors to reduce unit costs of development, production, production technology, purchasing, marketing and distribution.

YAMAHA

In 1970, Honda sold three times as many motorcycles as Yamaha. When Honda then turned its attention more to cars, Yamaha, which only made bikes, managed to reduce the gap between them, so that by 1979, Honda was now selling only 1.4 times as many bikes.

Yamaha then declared war on Honda in its statement by MD Hisao Koike:

> In a year, Yamaha will occupy first place in the domestic market. Furthermore, two years from now, Yamaha will be the world's top manufacturer of motorcycles.

When Honda got word of Yamaha's declaration of war, it intensified its product development efforts; in just one year, it introduced 40 new models.

Yamaha tried to stay in there as best it could. Prices on the motorcycle market fell dramatically, and some models were being sold at way below production cost in the fierce struggle to see who would be world leader— Honda or Yamaha.

The struggle turned into a war of attrition, in which financial resources would be the decisive factor. When Yamaha was forced to go to the banks to get loans to cover its losses, its chairman, Genichi Kawakami, decided to throw in the towel.

Yamaha publicly asked Honda's pardon for having presumed to try and take over its leading position in the motorcycle field, and the struggle was called off.

When the dust had settled, there were 2 million bikes in storage, Yamaha's MD had been fired and Suzuki had taken over second place.

(SOURCE: *Triad Power*, Kenichi Ohmae, Free Press)

OK

OK's unsuccessful frontal attack rapidly became a textbook example of encircling through counter-attack by the other side. The question is whether OK's competitors did not in the long term bring OK to its knees by combining low price levels (which OK had set as 'market leader') with invoice-tax-free account cards, cheaper cleaning, better service, better food service, etc.

94

Once again OK made the fatal mistake of regarding itself as acting as the market leader, but did not have the financial muscle required for a frontal attack. The best thing OK can do now is probably realize that it is weak and draw the conclusions from this in word and deed.

IBM

When IBM finally went into the personal computer (PC) market, this was done with the usual IBM methods:

- Large parts of the production of IBM's personal computers took place outside IBM.
- Programming was carried out by independent software suppliers, which meant that a wide range of good software was available after only a few months.
- Distribution was both through IBM's sales organization and through independent dealers.

Since its entry into the PC market was made from a position of real superiority in small and large computers, word-processing systems, terminals and printers, competitors were *forced*, irrespective of whether they made personal or larger computers, to make their products *IBM-compatible*.

Competitors were forced to make improvements in partial systems to IBM's integrated system and IBM *chose* the whole time what was to be the computer market standard (IBM compatible).

After IBM forces competitors to market IBM-compatible niche products, they will increase the product introduction rate, which will make it difficult for competitors to make their products compatible. Where they want fierce fighting, they will give volume discounts calculated on total purchases of IBMs in some key businesses.

The final blow for the competitors will be when the volume discounts become general, while at the same time it will be made very difficult or impossible for them to make their products IBM compatible.

A brilliant encirclement. Competitors will be forced to choose whether to fight at IBM's choosing or to make their own computers and challenge IBM. Two fights which are very difficult to win unless IBM nods off in its position as market leader.

ASEA'S ROBOT ACTIVITIES IN JAPAN

Extract from a strategic lecture in November 1984 by Bjorn Weichbrodt, ASEA Robotics:

95

ASEA Robotics currently comprises about 800 people all over the world, with a volume of about 750 million Swedish kronor in 1984, of which 90 per cent was invoiced outside Sweden, and a growth rate of 40–50 per cent a year.

Our activities comprise industrial robots with function packages and system solutions where the size of our systems and the client's undertakings vary.

From starting in Europe in 1974, we came to the conclusion in 1980 that long-term success would require active operations in both the USA and Japan. Japan currently represents almost 40 per cent of the world markets for industrial robot systems.

The aim of ASEA Robotics is to be one of the absolute leaders in the world in the field of industrial robotics and automation. This has already been converted to an aim of 30–35 per cent of the European market and a 20 per cent market share in the USA. As far as Japan is concerned, we set a target of 8–10 per cent of the market right from the start. This means that we will be one of the leading robotics companies in Japan, with operations including of course marketing, production and technical development.

Our definition of success in Japan, in addition to reaching this goal, is also to make long-term contacts with suppliers of components at competitive prices and quality and to learn Japanese production technology that we can adapt to other markets.

During the two years which have passed since the start, our operations have grown very quickly. We were able to establish a starting group by internal readjustments within Gadelius. We were also able to set aims. With Gadelius' weighty presence in Japan over the last 76 years, robotics activities have grown in two years to order books worth about 75 million kronor in 1983, which represents about 10 per cent of ASEA Robotics' total operations at present. Our rate of growth in Japan is now higher than in any other market.

ASEA Robotics in Japan currently has about 60 employees, robotics centres in Tokyo, Kobe and Nagoya and assembles robots at its own works in Kobe.

Market penetration by flank attack
To be successful, we must find a competitive advantage which can be understood by customers. Simply selling a standard product which already exists locally is something I believe to be very difficult. In our case, our activities are based first on our unique ability to adapt within certain fields which are already established in Japan, namely casting, cleaning, grinding, polishing, grading and other processing operations. This has been an important factor in our growth to date.

It is necessary to give our own troops simple, concrete aims. Selling a given number of robots in a year is an aim around which you can group your forces.

4. Bypass attack

If you are fighting a comparatively hard struggle on existing geographic brands or product areas, it is probably better to hold your positions in existing areas and either conquer new geographic markets or get into new product areas.

JAPAN INC

In February 1981, two American congressmen, John Danforth and Lloyd Bentsen, representing areas highly dependent on the American car industry, tabled a draft Bill which meant that no more than 1.6 million foreign cars could be imported a year. The Japanese car companies, led by Toyota, started a campaign against the proposed bill and pointed out, amongst other things, how many employees they had in the US, how much tax they paid and also how the content of US-produced components in their cars was rising continually.

Nissan's assistant MD, Yasuhiko Suzuki, stated that Americans bought Japanese cars because American car companies did not make anything like them and that as soon as American small cars came into existence, imports from Japan would fall.

'Imports have been drawn in to fill the "temporary" gap between domestic production and consumer demand for small cars,' he said. President Reagan's line, in conjunction with the Japanese foreign minister, Masayoshi Ito, was getting the Japanese to go along with voluntary import restrictions. Ito left the meeting with Reagan hoping to escape having to put his signature to any restriction on importing cars.

The chairman of the Senate finance committee, Bob Dole, later explained to the Japanese that they were considering restricting imports to less than

1.6 million cars. When Germany's foreign minister, Otto Lamsdorff, also warned the Japanese that if the US decided to act against imports of Japanese cars, Germany would follow suit, the Japanese gave way.

On 19 April 1981, MITI's chief, Rokusuke Tanaka, proposed a voluntary limitation of imports of Japanese cars to 1.68 million a year for two years, with the possibility of an increased import quota if the American car industry recovered in that time, together with a third limit on imports if both sides later agreed. The agreement was published on 1 May 1981.

Detroit's car industry had worked with Washington in these 'lateral manoeuvres' to create a breathing-space for American car producers to convert to more competitive products.

What the Japanese did once the Americans had joined forces against them was of course to try and find ways of *getting round* the agreement. There was an important part missing in the agreement, and that was the import limit set in terms of import *value*. So, instead of selling three Civics, Honda sold two Accords or Preludes instead, full of extras as standard equipment—and other Japanese car companies did the same.

The upgrading of their products which the Japanese had applied earlier to such things as motorcycles, clocks, outboard motors, hifi systems, cameras, TV and radio equipment once they felt truly established in a market had taken longer in the car industry, but now speeded up rapidly under the pressure of import restrictions. At the same time as the American car manufacturers were putting a great deal of effort and money into making smaller cars, they came face to face with the Japanese in their own traditional market segment.

The Japanese, who had been trying to prevent an agreement on restricting imports for a very long time, finally gave way, but because they were now selling larger cars with larger profit margins they were earning more than before on their exports to the USA.

The 'lateral manoeuvres', which the Japanese had lost at first sight, reduced the risk of further sanctions, that is the other side's freedom of action was tied down; and with the aid of the evasive action of selling larger and dearer cars, the Japanese regained the initiative and increased their freedom of action.

(MAIN SOURCE: *Car Wars*, Robert Sobel, Times Books)

HONDA

While Soichiro Honda—financed, amongst others, by Mitsubishi Bank and Mitsubishi Trust—was trying to establish himself as the world's leading motorcycle manufacturer, Honda began producing cars in 1962.

For Soichiro Honda, who had been heard to say, 'Driving a car is like sitting in the living room; driving a motorcycle is something like riding a horse—it's driving and controlling something that is almost alive,' it was natural that the first car was a small sports model—the S500.

In 1966, Honda brought out its new S800 sports car at the motor shows in London and Paris, and achieved good sales.

In 1968, when the smaller Japanese car companies were drawing up plans to attack the American market in the wake of Toyota and Nissan, Honda turned its attention instead to the European market with its new N600 small car, which was much smaller than the VW 'beetle'.

The main reason that Honda concentrated on Europe was they did not think themselves strong enough to survive on the American market, where competition was fierce. (Compare Honda's motorcycle efforts, where they concentrated on the US market first and only later on Europe, because their main opponents were the European motorcycle manufacturers—mainly the British—and the competition was therefore tougher in Europe.)

While the whole motor trade's attention was on Mazda's development of the Wankel motor, Honda developed the 'CVCC' motor, which was a development of the cylinder motor but with much better fuel economy and cleaner exhaust.

In 1970, Honda started selling the N600 on the American market, and in 1972, the Civic was introduced, with a powerful CVCC motor.

The Civic was the first Japanese car to be sold on its image as a quality car at a relatively high price, rather than a low-cost economy car. Honda now had the perfect technology (CVCC motor and small car experience) to take advantage of high petrol prices and increasing concern about the environment.

But what was the point, when petrol prices were low and car buyers were more interested in the Toyota Corolla, the Nissan PL620 and the Mazda Wankel-motored RX2 and RX3? In 1972, Honda sold only 20,500 cars, compared with Toyota's 327,000.

In 1973 came the first oil price shock, and by redesigning the Civic to make it more suited to the needs of the American market, Honda had the most economical car on the market in 1974, just when the demand was for cars of that type. When Toyota and Nissan raised their prices on the American market dramatically in 1974, Honda refused to follow suit.

While Toyota and Nissan were trying to become full-range manufacturers, Honda concentrated all its efforts on developing a single model—the Accord. This was introduced in the USA in 1976 and was a great success, with long waiting lists and high used prices as a result.

The Accord, which was loaded with extras, was marketed as a quality car at a premium price, with slogans like: 'The list of standard equipment starts where most lists end.' In this way, the Accord gained an image as a luxury car, which had a knock-on effect on the Civic, which was now bought by people who could not afford an Accord.

While other Japanese car companies rejected the idea of producing cars in the USA, Honda decided in 1979 to begin producing motorcycles near Columbus, Ohio.

In 1978, Honda introduced the Prelude sports car on the American market, and their sales rose while Toyota and Nissan were having problems selling their cars to the Americans, who were now preferring larger cars since their memory of the first oil crisis had faded.

When the second oil crisis came in 1979, it was very clear that Honda had been developing and marketing for a long time the cars which set the standard for the industry at the beginning of the 1980s.

In 1980, Honda sold 375,000 cars on the American market and could have sold over 500,000 if only they had the production capacity.

(MAIN SOURCE: *Car Wars*, Robert Sobel, Times Books)

5. Guerrilla attack

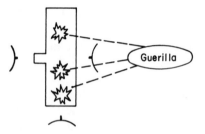

Guerrilla warfare often comes to mind when a weaker side is fighting against a stronger one; but even for the stronger side, using guerrilla strategy can have great advantages.

Act through lateral manoeuvres as in the example shown earlier. If necessary, call on the consumer ombudsman, environmentalists, the gutter press that like to see David taking on Goliath. Work with brand-name conflicts and anti-monopoly legislation. *In brief: appoint an environmental campaigner like Ralph Nader and some good lawyers.* It may be a question of presenting your company as a friendly company fighting against giant, insensitive, profit-hungry concerns. You must work continually at making selective price cuts, advertising campaigns, buying up key suppliers, courting dealers with poor back-up from competitors and so on.

'FIGHTING BRAND, FIGHTING COMPANY'

If you are fighting against competitors the bulk of whose activity is in other geographical markets or other business/product areas, it may be useful to have a monitoring operation there. If competitors then make aggressive efforts against your main market, you can activate your 'fighting brand' and use it as a negotiating plank in the important struggle for the main market.

This strategy is frequently a question of acting rapidly, unpredictably, giving pinpricks, forcing the other side to spread out its resources. The guerrilla works on the basis of a long war and avoids decisive struggles, aiming instead for localized victories. By concentrating his resources against the enemy's spread-out forces, the guerrilla gains the upper hand at local level so that different areas can be conquered one after the other.

Getting an agency in Japan or working with your Japanese competitor's worst rival in Japan can open up opportunities for successful guerrilla strategy.

CATERPILLAR

Caterpillar's most serious competitor on the world market, Komatsu, has been forced to discover that Caterpillar is working in Japan with the next-largest Japanese earth-moving equipment manufacturer.

Komatsu therefore finds harder competition in Japan, while Caterpillar is gaining a better understanding of the Japanese success formula and can apply it on international markets.

IKEA

In a number of advertisements, all variations on the same theme, the Swedish furniture company IKEA compared carefully selected IKEA products (lamps, bookcases, sofas, beds) with corresponding products from NK, the prestige department store. This technique of comparison can be illustrated using the ad for the Sultan luxury bed. It showed a big picture of a bed with the words:

5,195.—?
No, IKEA

Then came the biting text: 'No doubt you've seen the Expensive Shop's Fine Bed. For the sake of your back. For the sake of your sleep. But don't rush for your wallet, for now there is the Sultan luxury bed. The bed that's half the price of the Fine Bed, but at least just as good. We have the furniture-makers' word for that.

Sultan luxury bed is made in Sweden. It has the same kind of spiral springing system as the Fine Bed, which gives excellent support. But there the similarity ends.'

101

Then followed some striking comparisons:

Sultan luxury bed has a mattress which includes a 22 mm polyester layer, which gives firmness and comfort. In the Fine Bed, you'll find fibre filling and other things that are nice to lie on but which cost double the price and are impossible to clean or dry-clean.

The ad finishes with the following text:

Sultan luxury bed costs 2,575.—, the equivalent Fine Bed 5,195.—. (Move up in the world)
IKEA—Not for the rich. But for the clever.

Note: IKEA's main aim in the first wave of the attack with 'Exclusive shops on the fancy street' ad were undoubtedly to alter their 'low price—poor quality' image on the market (repositioning) and not taking customers from NK; but NK served as the butt, since everyone knew that NK stands for high quality.

NK

The Swedish NK group had not been doing well for some years. Competition had increased sharply, from such people as IKEA, which after its notable 'Exclusive shops on the fancy street' were now attacking NK indirectly by showing pictures of plush penthouse flats or stately homes with cheap IKEA furniture as a natural ingredient.

The advertising was aimed at NK's traditional circle of customers and their children, who were possibly just in the process of furnishing their housing co-op flat, and wanted the most fashionable surroundings, to give them something to think about. The message was: exclusive surroundings and inexpensive IKEA furniture go together (providing that you are not stuck in hidebound thought habits).

NK then went on to the counter-attack by taking on the head of IKEA's largest store on King's Curve, Stockholm. Horst Bohnke thus became the head of NK's largest store, on Hamngatan (Fancy street) in Stockholm. In this way, NK gained a skilful store chief, at the same time robbing IKEA of a key person—but also, into the bargain, many years' detailed knowledge of why IKEA is so successful, its strengths and weaknesses.

IKEA's period of 'easy victories' over NK is perhaps now over. Engaging competitors' key personnel is a common and very effective way of pursuing guerrilla warfare in the market, which the fast-growing 'head-hunting industry', amongst others, lives on.

ESSELTE AND DYMO

Extract from the strategic lecture 1982 by MD Sven Wallgren:

We were all clear at Esselte that if we were going to be really big in office equipment—and we were going to be—we would have to get a brand name. Dymo and Letraset were two of the bare half-dozen which could be found in all bookshops and stationers.

We decided on Dymo, and tried to negotiate for their Visual Systems Division, i.e. their marking pens and labelling equipment, which could be found in almost all stores. Since starting in 1959, the company had bought the German Meto, which was involved in price-tags and labels. Both activities were highly profitable, and in a few years Dymo was 'The darling of the New York stock exchange'.

Gradually, the Dymo board found that they had to do something with all their money. They decided to become, if not the world's biggest, then at least very nearly so in the field of computerized typesetting. But this was a dangerous business which cost unheard-of sums of money in itself, and partly involved tax complications which led to Dymo shares tumbling violently.

This was the situation when we made our first approach in the summer of 1977. In the autumn of the same year, we tried to force an acquisition by bypassing the board and offering the board chairman 31 million dollars for the Visual Systems Division. We hoped that—as the American government requires—they would be forced to go to the Stock Exchange and announce the bid. But they managed to get out of it—mainly with the assistance of lawyers who were cleverer than ours.

Good Friday

Then some months passed until, early on the morning of Good Friday at the beginning of April, I was woken by a telephone call from New York asking 'Are you still interested in Dymo Visual Systems?'

A few days later, two of our employees were on their way over the Atlantic to get all the information about Dymo which could be got over there, and on 12 May Esselte made an offer for all Dymo shares, an offer which was made direct to the shareholders. We knew that we would have no success with the management or the board. The offer was sent out on Sunday evening in the form of a four and a half page long text of an advertisement to be published the next morning and was therefore public to all intents. Out of politeness, the usual thing in this situation is to ring the chairman of the company and say, 'Read the *New York Herald Tribune* tomorrow—you'll find something interesting to read', and so that's what we did.

Then the storm quickly broke—roughly in the shape and size we had expected. It was all very dramatic.

Dymo was front-page news in the Stockholm papers for 11 days. I myself was summonsed before a court in New York for, amongst other things, having issued incorrect information in our 'Offer Document'. This was a delaying tactic, while they tried to find other ways out or at least push up the price.

All in all, we could have read everything that happened in advance on hostile takeover bids in the *Harvard Business Review*. I had already explained to the board and friends that there would be the nastiest things about Esselte and me personally in the American press, but even so some of my friends came and asked me what the hell I was doing.

For a month, until just after the acquisition, we had large numbers of lawyers and other specialists working shifts on the case. (The rest were shuttling over the Atlantic.) Bengt Strandberg flew back and forth over the Atlantic nine weeks in a row, I myself did this twice and was also involved, amongst other things, in keeping the Board up to date and having long talks every night with the people we had sent over.

So we rounded up the shares, got the crucial 50 per cent and then went on to 100 per cent. Some days later, the board resigned, which is part of the game. They were replaced by a new board of our choosing, and a new MD. This sounds terrible to Swedish ears, but is also part of the game.

Then we carried out a total integration of Dymo with Pendaflex. A number of Esselte subsidiaries in a number of countries suddenly had two of everything: two MDs, two warehouses, etc. In the USA, where Dymo was not a good name, it became Esselte Pendaflex, but in Europe, where it had a good resonance, it was joined together with Esselte and became a new company.

Esselte on the world map

The acquisition of Dymo put Esselte properly on the map amongst the big banks in the world and of course also in our industry. As far as I know, this is the only hostile takeover which a non-American company has brought off in the USA.

In 1979–80, Esselte had a very good result. We had benefited greatly from Dymo. It had a rather high margin type of product with very high marketing costs. We expected that our more anonymous Esselte products would be pulled along with it, which has in fact been the case.

H & M

The Swedish-owned low-price clothing chain Hennes & Mauritz, like IKEA, attacked NK, the up-market department store, in a series of advertisements and at the same time improved its own image. Here we show the most eye-catching ad. Two vivacious young people almost bursting with happiness at being alive take up most of the ad—and then comes the text:

Sorry, NK
And all the other stores who
know how to make money.

Excuse us for coming forward
with the first new Spring
fashions. The emerald green
suit with the long, wide
jacket for her. Jacket 298.—
skirt 169.—
And the pencil-grey linen
suit for him. Jacket 329.—,
trousers 249.—. Not very
polite, we know.
And the prices?
Completely ridiculous—we
agree. But isn't it worth it
just to be able to thumb our
noses a little at our finer
colleagues?

H & M
Not as silly as we look.

The H & M ad captures the heart of all guerrilla warfare: the guerrilla's superior morale. Here they present themselves as having a higher morale than NK. 'The customer' gets the impression that NK is incredibly expensive, in contrast to H & M.

NCR

Around 1900, NCR, the world leader in cash machines, came under competition from local companies who bought second-hand machines, repaired them, did them up and then sold them at much lower prices than NCR's new machines. They were also making a good living out of this, which annoyed John Patterson, NCR's MD, even more.

'The best way to kill a dog is to cut off its head,' said Patterson, and Thomas Watson was given the job of wielding the axe.

So Watson started up a company called Watson's Cash Register and Second-Hand Exchange, with the sole aim of putting an end to the competition from firms selling second-hand equipment. It was not necessary for him to make a profit: his success or failure would be judged by how many companies disappeared from the market. In Thomas and Marva Belden's biography of Watson, they tell how NCR set to work.

Watson set up shops opposite successful competitors, copied their recipe for success, avoided their mistakes, took on competitors' salespeople, and set his prices significantly lower than those of the competition.

In this way, Watson got the competition to throw in the towel, first in Manhattan, then in Philadelphia and Chicago. From Chicago, operations then spread out to cover the whole United States.

Watson was also involved in one of Patterson's favourite campaigns covering 'knock-out machines'—the so-called 'knockers'. NCR developed and advertised cash machines which were virtually copies of competitors' products, but at much lower prices. The idea was not in fact to sell these 'knockers', but simply to make the customers think twice before buying any machine that did not have 'NCR' on it.

If customers decided to buy a 'knocker' instead of a machine from NCR's normal range, NCR delayed delivery as long as it could, and finally sent a machine which did not do the job. The customer was then forced to change up to NCR's normal range, and NCR had succeeded in preventing the competition getting orders.

This last example is of particular interest, since IBM's competitors frequently complained that it was selling 'phantom computers'. These were machines which were soon to be in production, and, as IBM salesmen said, had a much better price/performance ratio than the computers Honeywell or CDC were currently trying to sell.

After finishing his work at NCR, Watson became the head of NTR (Computing—Tabulating—Recording), which changed its name in 1924 to International Business Machines (IBM).

(SOURCE: *IBM—Colossus in Transition*, Robert Sobel, Times Books)

Burnt grass

Extract from strategy lecture by MD Sverker af Winklerfelt, CAD Partner, Stockholm.

Burning the grass around you was originally a method of reducing the effect of the Indians' fire arrows and preventing a concealed advance.

In marketing warfare, 'Burnt Grass' is used as a method of burning the other side's arguments and actions. It can also lead to the other side being confused and demoralized.

The 'Burnt Grass' strategy makes great demands on the user, whose own arguments and actions must always be adapted to the moment, so as to be always one step ahead of the other side. It cannot therefore be used without an effective intelligence service. It is not enough to know the other side's general sales strategy—its psyche must also be known. Of course this works best if one knows the other side's sales personnel, even down to sales level. It is also important to know the other side's decision-making model.

Your own salesforce must be given a good training in tactics if this is to work in the field. The method may prove (or should be)

106

unethical, but you must be aware that dirty tricks can occur to protect yourself against them. The choice and force of arguments and measures is therefore largely a question of morals. Dirty methods can damage a company's image, and even if they can win battles, you cannot be certain that they will win the war.

The precondition for effective application of 'Burnt Grass' tactics is an oligopoly situation with few, known competitors who can be observed and analysed. 'Burnt Grass' can be used in connection with the launching of something new—a product or a company—in an *established* market. Used correctly, the method means that what the competitor recognizes as one's weaknesses become strengths and the competitor's strengths are used again and turned into weaknesses.

Some scenarios:

1. A NEW COMPANY

You want to start a new company (or a branch office) in an established market, where you have identified your main competitor, who has been there a long time and has a well-established position. You know that this competitor will use its size and market position against you.

Some casually said arguments:

- Of course we are small today on this market. We are bringing a new concept to the market and the benefit of our size is that we can quickly adapt to your requirements.
- Our modern new approach to this traditional market has already been shown to be successful. Customers like the alternative to a big and *expensive* vendor living on yesterday's performance. We do not talk about yesterday—we talk about tomorrow!

2. PRICING

You are launching a new product and you know that your competitor—the big market leader—will give hefty discounts to maintain its market share.

If you know that the competitor will give up to say 25 per cent discount to major customers, you can tell them that you know cases where *really important* customers will get about 40 per cent and the rest at least 30 per cent.

Some other remarks:

- It is bad for everyone's business that they are so desperate. What will you say when you find out that your own competitor can get the same products for a lower price?
- It's always a question of survival in the long run. Even an elephant needs food!

3. WINING AND DINING

You know that your competitor will offer your prospective customer a slap-up dinner at the end of the sales cycle. You have to find out the exact date—and if possible even the restaurant. 'Burnt Grass' gives you some alternatives:

(A) You cannot do it yourself the evening before the event. Let the customer understand that your company certainly is not going to cover bad products by expensive wining and dining. Indicate why you have a firm policy on pricing and 'after all who is paying for it in the end?'

(B) Exclusive-elegant dinner. You take the customer out for dinner the evening before. You bring him to a restaurant with good food and drink. You let him understand that the ethical rules of your company do not allow overspending and that you personally find that morally dubious. You should take great care over the food and the wines and avoid spirits. Try to make a mental link between drinking alcohol and being 'bought'!

In the same way that your customer appreciates your care with the wines, the following evening lands him in a moral dilemma, which should wreck the evening for the other side.

In addition, after 'your' dinner your customer comes home early and sober—which is usually appreciated by the family.

(C) Slap-up dinner—yourself! You invite your customer to a slap-up dinner with all the trimmings. In addition, you keep him as late as possible and with as much alcohol as possible.

The next day is difficult for him. Your competitors have a job getting through, and if they insist they meet with irritation. Their evening will be at best a half-hearted repeat performance.

The reaction from the customer's family will definitely not help the competition. They can cope with one evening, but hardly with two in a row.

> *A commander should say to himself several times a day: if the enemy's army appears in front of us on our left or right flank—what would I do? 'If he cannot answer the question immediately, his planning is poor, something is wrong. He must correct his mistake quickly.'*
> (Napoleon)

Defence strategies

A great deal that applies to attacking strategies also holds good for defence. The greatest effect will probably be achieved by combing different defence strategies.

7. Position defence

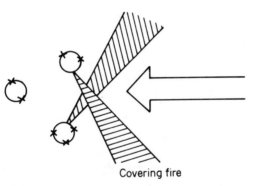

Covering fire

The idea of defence is closely tied to fortifications and fieldworks; but successful defence strategy must always have sufficient depth and exploit all the advantages of the terrain. The enemy's attack must be warded off through a system of fixed positions with a coordinated fire system. There must be freedom of action so that one can go over to the defensive when the time seems most favourable.

Positional defence in business means using all one's resources to consolidate one's position within existing market/product segments. This often happens under pressure of stiff competition (see SKF example), or major structural change (e.g. the drop in oil consumption, see the Exxon example). The management literature bestseller of 1983, *In Search of Excellence* says that the companies which stick to what they know and avoid the temptation of diversifying their activities are among the most successful in the USA.

SKF

At the beginning of the 1970s, SKF, the Swedish ball-bearing company, found itself involved in a life-and-death struggle with Japanese ball-bearing manufacturers supported by MITI, and carried out a textbook example of positional defence. From among SKF's 50,000 varieties of bearings, the Japanese decided to enter the European market in the first instance with the large-volume bearings (about 500 out of the 50,000) and dropped the price by 20 per cent.

SKF then implemented the GFSS project (officially begun in 1973) which involved:

- Reduction of the range from 50,000 to 20,000 types.
- Production of each type at *one* factory only (SKF had factories in Sweden, England, Germany, France and Italy).

The increase in volume enabled better production equipment to be used for 'series' instead of 'batch' production, faster capital turnover and a cost level which dropped from 100 to 40.

SKF won the war of attrition by concentrating on the essentials and where it was strongest, and the Japanese offensive in Europe was stopped. The Japanese currently have 4 per cent of the European ball-bearing market.

ELECTROLUX

Extract from a strategic lecture by group chief Gosta Bystedt in 1982:

15 years ago, the Electrolux group's turnover was around the billion mark, with 20,000 employees, 40 subsidiaries and 6 production lines. The corresponding figures for 1981 were a turnover of 26 billion, 100,000 employees, 389 subsidiaries and 29 production lines, if Gränges is counted as a production line.

Although the 1960s were one of the best decades in world history in economic terms, Electrolux's sales and results were stagnant, because of unfavourable production facilities, high administrative and distribution costs and increasing competition in white goods, i.e. refrigerators, freezers, dishwashers and washing machines.

It was mainly the Italians who had overcome the aftermath of the war and built up new, large, effective factory units with the aim of going out and conquering the world with low prices.[1]

Our risks were also spread unfavourably, since in fact we only had one product which gave decent results, namely the WennerGrens vacuum

---

[1] Compare the acquisition of Zanussi and how the roles were exchanged.

cleaner. Its direct selling methods were only suited to vacuum cleaners, but were also used for white goods, since there was a great shortage of specialist dealers. And white goods were loss-makers in direct selling. Direct selling encourages cost-effectiveness less than effectiveness at selling. The former was very low compared with what could be achieved in mechanized distribution.

Fortunately we got Hans Werthen as MD when things were at their bleakest (he arrived in 1967). I myself was then making a good living as manager of the successful vacuum cleaner division.

Among the guidelines we set up were rationalization, organizational simplification and cost-reducing drive.

Sales companies just sell

We asked ourselves, 'What sort of units need what sort or organization?' Not infrequently, a complete set-up with functions and experts is required. So we organized sales companies on the domestic side so that all they had to do was to sell and also buy all services—personnel, finance, warehousing, transport, servicing. This cut costs enormously. But the secret is then to see that these service-selling functions do not become bureaucratic and ineffective. We did the same thing on the factory side, and now we have a number of satellite factories which also purchase services.

This is something we are always involved in. We are very much involved in questions of construction and mechanization of production. What are dominant in Electrolux are the mature products, our innovatory phase is behind us, and there is a risk of over-production, even for household products. It is a question of squeezing prices by mechanizing, robotization, standardization, longer series runs and greater volume to get on anything like an equal footing with the international competitors.

Company acquisition

We also needed to rationalize our structure, but for this aim also, volume was required if it was to be profitable, and company acquisition was the answer.

EXXON

Exxon is now unchallenged as the world's largest company. Its total turnover of around 85 billion pounds in 1984 easily exceeded the Gross National Product of Sweden and most other countries. In the last decade, Exxon has spent 40 billion pounds on investments, mostly in oil prospecting and production. For 1984 alone, investments amounted to 8 billion pounds.

Staying in Europe

Even a company like Exxon is affected by the market if forces in the outside world are sufficiently great. And this has in fact been the case in recent years, with falling oil prices, falling sales and overcapacity. But while other oil companies are responding by withdrawing from Europe and buying up competitors to get at cheap oil reserves, Exxon has taken the opposite way.

Exxon's response instead was to show even more clearly its interest in staying in Europe, at the same time carrying out major restructuring of activities downstream, such as marketing, distribution and refineries, and in putting even more effort into activities upstream, such as production and oil exploration.

'The difference between us and the companies who withdrew from Europe is that we have a much stronger position there. The fact is that, together with Shell, we are the strongest company on the European market and that we will continue to hold this position in future,' says Dick Kruizenga of Exxon.

Decline in the market

Exxon has managed to retain its competitiveness in Europe by thorough-going restructuring, which began in 1981 and is still not yet complete.

'The decline in the market was very dramatic. From being a 5-million-barrel-a-day company aiming at being a 6-million-barrel-a-day company, we went down to 4 million. So we adapted the organization to what the market was actually doing instead of what we expected it to do. We have made some progress here, but there is still some tidying up to be done,' says Kruizenga.

Up to the present time, Exxon has closed two refineries, 14,000 petrol stations and (mainly through retirement and natural wastage) the workforce has dropped by 24,000 from its peak of 180,000. Tanker capacity has also been reduced by sales and scrapping by 25 per cent, or 5 million dwt. The fleet continues to lose nearly a billion Sek a year, however.

Out of this trauma, a company has emerged which is far more cost-effective than before. The key word in this process was 'concentration', and mainly where Exxon can really achieve this: in drilling for, producing and selling gas, oil and oil products.

Exxon's oil exploration costs amount to 6 dollars a barrel—a figure which is only beaten by Mobil. And in three of the past five years Exxon has succeeded in finding more oil than the company produces, a result which not many in the industry can match.

(SOURCE: Carl Johan Johard, Sweden's *Business Week*, no 3/85)

8. Mobile defence

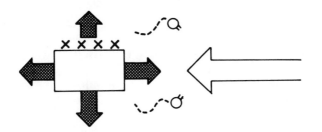

Mobile defence is a strategy which in military terms has been developed in recent times. A high degree of mobility in defence prevents the attacker's chances of localizing defence and accumulating its forces for a decisive battle. Mobile defence is conducted over wide areas and with highly mobile mechanized units. The idea is to avoid holding ground *unnecessarily*. NATO's strategy for the defence of Central Europe is built to a great extent on flexible defence.

By analysing the functional requirements ('generic need') which we and others satisfy in the market and not being hypnotized by existing products, new possibilities can be opened up.

In his famous article 'Marketing Myopia' (*Harvard Business Review*, 1960), Theodore Lewitt describes how American railroad companies went bankrupt because they thought they were in the railway industry and did not realize they were in the *transportation* industry. Instead of putting all their resources into existing market/product segments, they should have invested in new market/product segments while they were still profitable.

By widening your business concept, you can see opportunities which you wouldn't have seen otherwise.

Expanding into neighbouring market/product segments where synergy can be achieved between the old and the new gives companies a much greater depth of strategy.

ASEA

ASEA, with super-strategist Percy Barnevik at the helm, has just finished redefining ASEA from full-range supplier in the power field to power company, which has competitive advantages within the product niches.

ASEA is concentrating on expansive fields of application such as:

- power;
- mass transport;
- automation.

The basis for this effort is thoroughgoing research in power and industrial technology and materials development.

With this achievement, ASEA has succeeded in being the world leader in such diverse fields as:

- coal-fired boilers with fluid bed technology;
- high voltage DC;
- industrial robots;
- thyristor locomotives.

It has achieved this by dividing its activities logically into strategic business units (SBUs) and having a central control which can see the synergic effects between different commercial fields.

Let us quote from the annual report for 1984:

In spite of the wide variety of fields where it is involved, ASEA is characterized by great technological cohesion. Our thorough-going technical developments are used in a large number of fields. Components such as thyristors, microcomputers, etc. are used in different products and in our various fields of operations.

Large-scale use of our own products and components enables rational production, at the same time giving us an adequate basis for our development costs. Our own profile products enable us to be very competitive in building installations. Some examples:

- Industrial robots. In addition to knowledge from our own production facilities, robotics is based on ASEA's electronics and transmitters, strong new lightweight materials in mechanics and user-friendly software for man-machine communication.
- Locomotive development is based on new power electronics and microcomputer-based control systems. New materials in such things as bogies and wheels have been of decisive importance in better riding characteristics, and systems technology has been used in optimizing locomotives and complete trainsets.
- Competitiveness in handling large electrical loadings such as high-voltage DC is based on power electronics, new materials and systems technology with simulation of installations.

This example of flexible defence is at the same time a description of a company which is working 'on the internal lines'.

ELECTROLUX

Extract from strategy lecture by group chief Gosta Bystedt in 1982:

When it comes to increasing risk-spreading, diversification—trying to get more products—is one way, and one which in this respect we would choose even in preference to takeovers. Developing new products from nothing is like sowing a seed and waiting for a shoot. We chose to buy at least seedlings in the form of companies or licensing or cooperation agreements.

To spread the risks still further, it is of course necessary to spread distribution beyond direct sales: this is a question of increasing the specialist trade and was also achieved by buying companies. We made a few such large takeovers, for example the Arthur Martin group and Tornado in France which gave us a 20–25 per cent share of the French market.

Other examples are Progress in West Germany and Eureka, which increased our share of these markets significantly.

But while takeovers increase the risk-spreading, they are risky since it is a question of moulding each new company in the group style and being able to retain market shares, keeping key personnel and creating cooperation which helps our group interest. There is no point in takeovers if you just pile things up against one another: there have to be structural effects.

The worst mistake you can make in a takeover is not being objective. If there are good people in the company taken over, they must be taken in hand. It can easily happen that they feel themselves treated unjustly, and if you give them reason to feel that way, that is about the worst obstacle to success you can create. The entire success depends on the people involved not starting to trip each other up but marching in the same direction.

Turnover up 24 per cent a year
To sum up, therefore, we can say that the group's development over the last 15 years has been characterized by expansion, diversification and restructuring.

The average increase in turnover during the period—measured in terms of current prices—increased by 24 per cent a year, of which just on half came from takeovers and the rest through natural growth.

With only natural growth, which was 11 per cent a year during the period, turnover would have been about 5 billion instead of 26. Without takeovers, and with risk-spreading unchanged, the group would have found it hard to survive.

So takeovers have been wholly necessary for the group to be able to reduce its risk exposure fairly rapidly through structural improvement. It is very difficult, not to say impossible, to improve your structure effec-

115

tively when your base volume is inadequate. The companies taken over brought with them production volume which enabled factories to be specialized by interchanging products. At the same time, the group's market position has been strengthened by the fact that the market shares of the companies acquired have been retained almost without exception.

A large number of acquisitions, as has been said, were aimed at a broader product base and secondly to expanded distribution.

During the period 1981–3, they consolidated and reinforced their position, which involved sales of companies such as Facit and the disposal of assets.

ESSELTE

Extract from strategy lecture by group chief Sven Wallgren, 1982:

A new strategy

Since 1983, we have found a new strategy. We told ourselves that we were already where we wanted to be in the business field—in some respects possibly more than was desirable—but not in all the markets where we should be strong. So we rapidly created operations in Australia, Spain, Finland and France as complementary to the small companies we already had in those countries. Then we complemented these divisions with new products, for example by buying a binding works in Malmö and one in Lidingö and a sheet metal cabinet works in Smaland.

In the United States, many of our sales were through specialist office equipment dealers. But individuals and small companies bought these goods in department stores, where we had no sales strength. We tried to change this through Pendaflex, which had a separate programme for sales to consumers. We also bought a big manufacturer of photograph albums, which of course also ran along the same lines.

Our aim was thus to put together by purchases a sufficient volume of business to be able to become a force to be reckoned with in sales of office goods to department stores.

When we bought Dymo, we were already beginning to think that its labelling tapes would gradually be replaced by printing direct onto packaging, which led us to the question: should we shrink with a shrinking market—or should we say to ourselves that the 950 salespeople which Meto has around the world are a resource which should be used for something else?

We chose the latter strategy, and are now filling Meto with new products, such as electronic scales and queueing tickets. These are not products which are sold through the retail trade, but are used by retailers in their own rational operations.

9. Pre-emptive attack (offensive defence)

Offensive defence is a strategy which is based on the idea that it is better to pre-empt an expected attack by a competitor by attacking oneself. Attack is the best form of defence, as the saying goes.

The entire arsenal of alternative attack strategies is available here. The aim is to keep the initiative continuously and hence to force the competition on to the defensive.

Offensive defence is often used when a competitor gets a higher market share than is thought tolerable.

IBM

It was clear that third-generation computers were on the way by the late 1950s or early 1960s. This was due to the same technological factors which had created the second-generation machines: developments in technology and increasing competition in the computer industry.

Bell Laboratories and Texas Instruments were amongst the leaders when it came to developing integrated circuits—'computers on a chip'. As with a great deal of other research in the USA, it was a military project (Apollo and Minuteman) which was the driving spur.

Mass-production of integrated circuits meant the end of the road for computers based on transistors (the second-generation), and the birth of third-generation machines. Like its competitors, IBM was aware of this, but its massive investment in third-generation machines (the 360 series) was due partly to attacks by the competition, and partly to internal conflicts within IBM.

The competition
Honeywell had developed a range of computers with which to go on to the frontal attack against IBM's 1400 series. The H-200 computer could use the 1400 series software, and was faster, more powerful and yet cheaper than the IBM machines.

Control Data (CDC) had developed its 3600 series, which would win easily in any comparison with IBM's 7090, and was working on developing the 6600 series which was faster and more powerful than anything IBM could come up with.

117

Internal conflicts

IBM's overseas organization, World Trade, had become too independent for the liking of the IBM management in Armonk, USA. Together with the fact that IBM's medium-range (1400 series) and large (7000 series) computers were beginning to resemble one another to the point where the two separate sales organizations, the General Products and Data Systems divisions, frequently found that they were fighting one another rather than the competition, this led to IBM placing all its bets on one gigantic development project.

A decision was made in favour of a joint development project co-ordinated by IBM (USA)'s management (IBM Domestic) and with sales via a single marketing organization.

The project was led by Learson, Amdahl and Williams, and called SPREAD (Systems Programming, Research, Engineering And Development Committee).

Since the third-generation machines were not compatible with IBM's second-generation ones, they were forced to develop new software and peripherals for the 360 series. The decision also meant cannibalizing the 1400 and 7000 series—which seemed hopelessly outdated once the 360 series was introduced.

All this cost a great deal of money. It was reckoned that the final total would be twice that of the Manhattan project which developed the atomic bomb. Six major factories were built to manufacture the electronic components, and over a 5-year period the workforce increased by 50,000 people. Assembly-line production was introduced into the computer industry for the first time, and a greater percentage of components were developed by IBM itself than ever before.

IBM took on a number of lawyers who had been involved in actions by individual states against IBM for restraint of competition in order to be able to handle all the actions for unfair competition, monopoly, etc. which competitors were expected to bring when the 360 series was introduced.

After a large number of failures and delays, the 360 series was introduced in 1965 and was an overnight success. Less than two years later, the 360 series represented half the total value of IBM installations in the USA, and its already high market share increased still further. Playing for high stakes had paid off.

Watson's aim had been to produce a technologically superior family of computers, expand into new market segments, keep the competition out and unify his company. He succeeded in most of these aims, at the same time changing the face of the whole computer industry.

(SOURCE: *IBM—Colossus in Transition*, Robert Sobel, Times Books)

118

VOLVO CARS

Extract from 1982 lecture by Hakan Frisinger:

We began in 1975 by looking at our total system and saw that rapid offensive moves would have to be made if we were to survive. On the industrial side, we had to achieve a massive increase in productivity and thorough-going increase in quality as quickly as possible.

We selected a survival strategy which meant managing and developing existing assets with the aid of aggressive surprise methods and tight operational control. Some examples:

- *Productivity development*: 1975–80 was 6 per cent, 1981 was 11 per cent.
- *Quality development*: where we achieved the aim of being comparable with the best in our class of cars.
- *Capital rationalization*: which dropped the average throughput of cars from 15 weeks to 10, releasing 800 million kronor in capital.

But the big challenge was to reach viable profitability, and here we needed not only cost reductions but also increased receipts.

What products should we develop?
Our approach was to create a Product Planning Division and a Construction and Development Division. This was a clear step towards customer- and product-orientation.

We rapidly saw that our resources were too small over the whole product development process, the so-called pre-production process. The financial attitude to product development meant that it went up from 5 per cent of turnover to the level we were counting on in the 1980s, that is 9–10 per cent, which in the context of the industry can be described as aggressive.

The strategy was an aggressive commitment to organization and product. We took on development personnel, poured in money and pushed an aggressive development project. We were able to do this since we had managed to survive by operating effectively, which gave us a positive cash-flow.

The decisive struggle was achieving viable profitability with the aid of strategic control. For strategic control to succeed, it is necessary to identify conditions in the industry, business opportunities and threats that exist. The next step is to formulate a programme of measures and finally carry them out.

The aim is to convince all those involved at Volvo that what we are doing is right, giving us long-term local loyalty and support for the daring strategy and for our product development project.

119

One tool that we use a great deal throughout our organization to convince people and get support for our products is our Perception Map—our characteristic diagram (Figure 39).

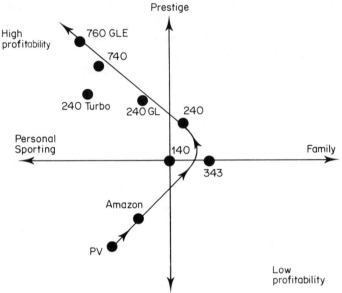

Volvo s North West strategy (characteristic diagram, completed after the lecture)

Figure 39

10. Counter-attack

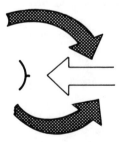

Counter-attack is a question of taking the initiative and going on to the attack in a situation where one is under attack oneself. It is therefore a question of exploiting the other side's weaknesses where this may involve an attack on defended terrain. The principle can be illustrated with the famous Finnish counter-strategy during the Winter War:

- Don't meet the enemy head-on.
- Let them force their way in and be thinned out.
- Concentrate resources on knocking out one unit at a time.
- Attack lines of communication and split them.
- Use the terrain to your advantage.

By letting a competitor's attack really get underway, we can see weaknesses in his methods in attacking markets and us. These may frequently be a segment which he has not managed to satisfy, or one he has forgotten, or something in his marketing mix which is not competitive. Perhaps his product has not the guarantees required or has a poor service organization, perhaps there are no spares, and so on.

This is where our big chance is of using the force of his attack against him, as in ju-jitsu. The harder they come, the harder they fall.

DOCKSIDE

The Dockside company, which makes deck shoes, says something like this in its advertisements.:

The trouble with comparing old Dockside shoes with the inumerable copies is that there aren't any old copies around.

The more competitors advertise, the harder Dockside's ad hits them.

SMIRNOFF

Smirnoff, Heublein's well-known brand-name vodka, had established a quality image worldwide through large-scale advertising and pro- motional activities. Suddenly, it was attacked by Wolfschmidt, which went on to the frontal attack by pricing its vodka, which was as good as Smirnoff's, a dollar lower in the hope of taking a share of the market from them.

The natural reaction on Smirnoff's part would have been to meet Wolfschmidt's lower price with a price reduction of its own and rely on Smirnoff's quality image being the decisive factor in a long war of attrition. Instead, they acted in the following, completely surprising way:

- They raised the price of Smirnoff by a dollar to reinforce in the minds of vodka consumers the difference in quality between other brands of vodka, and Wolfschmidt above all.
- They introduced two new brands of vodka which were priced the same as Wolfschmidt and a dollar lower respectively.

The result was that vodka consumers now had three Heublein vodkas to choose from and only one Wolfschmidt. In its counter-attack, Heublein attacked Wolfschmidt both frontally and from the flank—something that Wolfschmidt could never have expected in its worst nightmares.

MINERAL WATER

The Swedish milk marketing authorities had just finished their 'milk is life' campaign with sweet pictures of animals suckling their young. The mineral water manufacturers replied with the following ad:

Time to slaughter a holy cow?
The Board of Health thinks we Swedes ought to change our eating habits.

We eat too much fatty food, for example, and on top of that we drink fat in the form of milk. Of course, milk is a good drink for children and growing young people.

But a 25-year-old who regularly drinks milk with his food should perhaps think again. And the older you get, the less reason there is to drink a lot of milk. Your need for calcium and fat is more than satisfied by the food we eat, and nowadays milk has by no means the importance from a nutritional standpoint that it once had.

Change your habits and change from milk to mineral water now and then!

Carbonated mineral water is completely calorie-free and is the perfect mealtime drink. It doesn't clash with the taste of the food, enhances it. The Swedes drink on average only 7 litres of mineral water a year as against 150 litres of milk, so we will have to be good and take the narrow way. Those who claim that milk is life are wrong. It is water which is life!

Drink mineral water!

This ad is an example of counter-attack using guerrilla tactics aimed at repositioning the competition. The poor milk drinkers thought that milk was life, while in fact water is!

11. Flank positioning defence

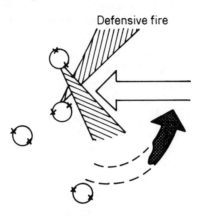

Defensive fire

Flank defence is a special form of positional defence, aimed at reinforcing otherwise vulnerable flanks and if possible creating the conditions for going over to a counter-attack.

Here it is a question of strengthening a weak product segment, for example, so that the competition does not bother to try and attack us or reinforce a segment already under attack. If we then become really strong, we can attack their flank by such things as launching a string of products in rapid succession, or cutting prices drastically or, if our quality is superior, giving a generous guarantee. In military parlance this is called 'outflanking' the other side. By stopping the competition's flank attack, we prevent them from exploiting their victories (bridgehead) to attack (penetrate) our main sector, which is their actual aim.

ALFA LAVAL

At the beginning of the 1980s, the Swedish company Alfa Laval, the world leader in marine separators, suddenly found its smaller separators coming under stiff competition from various Japanese companies, particularly in Asia.

Had Alfa Laval done what European and American motorcycle, camera and wristwatch manufacturers had done, they would have given Asia up lock, stock and barrel to the Japanese and concentrated in Europe and the States on the larger but more tailor-made separators where Alfa Laval's profits lay. What would have happened then is easy to imagine for anyone who has studied Japan's onslaught on the world in those fields.

123

In those fields, the Japanese quickly gave themselves the advantages of large-series economy within mass markets, gradually extended their distribution network and gained a good image of producing high-quality products at low prices.

They were able to do this more or less undisturbed, while their European and American counterparts climbed up the product ladder towards more expensive and exclusive products (upgrading), but unfortunately also with smaller and smaller market segments. Their reasoning was often, 'We can't compete with these guys who pay one-tenth the wages!'

When the Japanese had then built up their fighting potential by conquering the mass markets, they attacked their European and American competitors in their main sectors.

Alfa Laval, which had learnt from the mistakes of its colleagues, decided to use its size in marine separators and did what the motor cycle, camera and wristwatch makers should have done while their Japanese competitors were still relatively weak. Despite the protests of their workforce, they moved their production of smaller separators from Sweden to Japan to be nearer the market and keep a better eye on their Japanese competitors, at the same time taking advantage of the Japanese efficiency of production in terms of both their suppliers and their own installations.

ELECTROLUX'S PURCHASE OF ZANUSSI

Electrolux's white goods range covers the following fields:

- Cookers
- Freezers/fridges
- Dishwashers
- Cleaners
- Microwave ovens
- Kitchen accessories

In the first two areas, they are strong on the European market; otherwise, the position varies.

By taking over the Italian company Zanussi, Electrolux gained access amongst other things to the white-goods company Zanussi Elettro Domestici Spa with 8 factories and 12,800 employees.

The takeover meant that it:

- increased its *world domination* on the cooker market;
- complemented its high-quality refrigerators and freezers with Zanussi's medium-quality ones, achieving *market domination of the entire fridge/freezer market*;
- gained access to Zanussi's *domination of the washing machine market*;
- improved its position in the dishwasher market.

In 1983, the company's volume of various key products looked like this:

	Electrolux	Zanussi	Total
Vacuum cleaners	5,936,000	—	5,936,000
Fridges/freezers	1,882,000	2,445,000	4,327,000
Cookers	1,227,000	500,000	1,727,000
Washing machines	356,000	1,145,000	,1,501,000
Dishwashers	200,000	235,000	435,000
Microwave ovens	536,000	—	536,000
Oven hobs	222,000	—	222,000
TOTAL	10,359,000	4,325,000	14,684,000

Even in geographical terms, the advantages of coordination are great. Electrolux controls the North and is number one in France. Zanussi is strong where Electrolux has been weak up to now, for example in West Germany, Benelux and obviously in Italy. The company is reasonably well-placed in Austria, Spain and France.

(SOURCE: Electrolux annual report 1983, Sweden's *Business Week* no. 34/83, Mats Edman, Sweden's *Business Week*, no. 3/85)

12. Strategic retreat

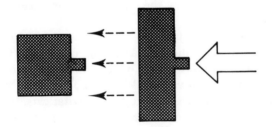

Many companies which had started diversifying in the 1960s and early 1970s under the influence of Theodore Lewitt's article 'Marketing Myopia' were to regret it at the end of the 1970s, and then began reconcentrating their resources on their old business field. The retreat also enabled economic action behind the lines.

ASEA

ASEA gave up its full-range policy and concentrated on the product sector where they could build up competitive advantage in the long term. Its entry into the international field, which was the next step in Percy Barnevik's transformation of the company, could now take place on a well-consolidated base.

CHRYSLER

Lee Iacocca took over at Chrysler in autumn 1978. One of his first actions was to ensure that he had a management team he could trust, which in practice meant bringing them over en masse from Ford to fill the top positions at Chrysler.

The long list of problems facing Chrysler increased with the second oil-price shock at the beginning of 1979. This time, the Japanese were sitting on the quayside at San Diego and Baltimore with 700,000 unsold small cars, and the situation was the same for the American small cars on the market. At the same time, there were long waiting lists for large cars with V8 motors, and American manufacturers were working overtime to keep up with demand.

All this changed overnight. The Japanese got rid of their 700,000 unsold small cars in 2 months, in many cases at far over the list price, while sales of large cars were halved. Rapid, drastic action was needed if Chrysler was to survive.

In his book *Iacocca*, Iacocca says that he felt like a military surgeon in a front-line hospital forced to decide who to save and who to let die.

Chrysler was forced to shut down 10 plants for good. In collaboration with the industry union (AUW), the number of employees was reduced by over 30 per cent.

Iacocca started by cutting his own salary from 360,000 dollars to one dollar, then he went further and cut the salaries of higher officials by 10 per cent. Then Iacocca went to the union, which had always had the impression that the management had always had it far too good (fat cats), and said, 'Well, now you're looking at some pretty skinny fat cats, OK? So what do you have to say?' According to Iacocca, from that moment he was on best terms with the union, which made it easier to get them to go along with a wage cut of two dollars an hour.

Chrysler cut stockholdings in all areas, and instead of making deliveries by lengthy freight train as before, turned to making deliveries by truck, which came many times a day. They even went as far as making the new K cars shorter, so they could get more of them on to a car carrier. The once-glossy annual report was replaced with one that was as simple as possible: black-and-white, on recycled paper, partly to save money, but also to give the shareholders the message that Chrysler really was doing everything it could to cut costs.

Chrysler sold its fortresses in the USA, and the Venezuelan operation was sold to GM. Its operations in Brazil and Argentina were sold to Volkswagen, the European operations to Peugeot. When all the sales had been

126

made, all that was left were the operations in the USA, Canada and Mexico. But that was not enough: Chrysler was forced to sell its most profitable division—the combat vehicle division, with the famous MI tank—to General Dynamics for 348 million dollars.

Nor did Iacocca have any qualms about getting rid of Chrysler's large staff, since he thought that the only way of staying efficient in a staff job was to deserve it by long line service. But Chrysler, like Ford, had a tendency to take on staff personnel with a college qualification as their only merit. Iacocca had little time for such merit lists; and many staff went.

Three years later, Chrysler had dropped the break-even point from 2.3 to 1.1 million dollars.

(MAIN SOURCE: Lee Iacocca, *Iacocca*, Bantam Books)

11 Choosing a strategy for the marketing war

The eleven different methods of conflict (strategies) which have been outlined in the previous chapter in principle cover the whole field of possible strategies in marketing warfare. The options can be split up still further if desired. The alternatives as described provide a complete basis for considering or selecting a strategy overall; but the alternative chosen must obviously be worked out in detail before it is put into operation.

The strategies between which we have to choose are as in Figures 40 and 41.

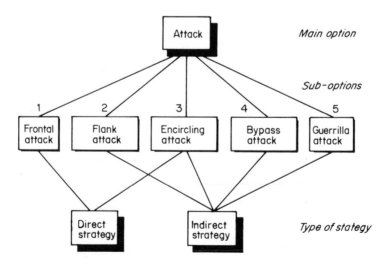

Figure 40

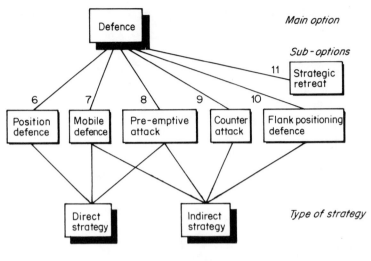

Figure 41

The methods of military strategy evaluation are described in more detail in Chapter 12, The decision-making process. The same methodology can be applied to marketing warfare. The choice of strategy must be made against the background of the positions you and the competition occupy in the market. The choice depends, amongst other things, on the market situation as a whole, the company's role in the market, its economic strength and assumed development options.

The BCG model

In its 'Growth Share Matrix', the Boston Consulting Group launched a model (the BCG model) which can help us define the strategic situation as a whole and hence aid us in the choice of strategy. In this section, we discuss and develop the BCG model and establish the strategic situations that can occur.

The product we are marketing is therefore placed in the matrix in relation to the market rate of growth and our own market share (Figure 42). The model then tells us which strategic situation overall applies to the product in question.

The products in square I are a company's main products (so called 'cash cows') with good profitability and positive cashflow. The highest priority is always to keep the cashcows' positions and defend their competitiveness.

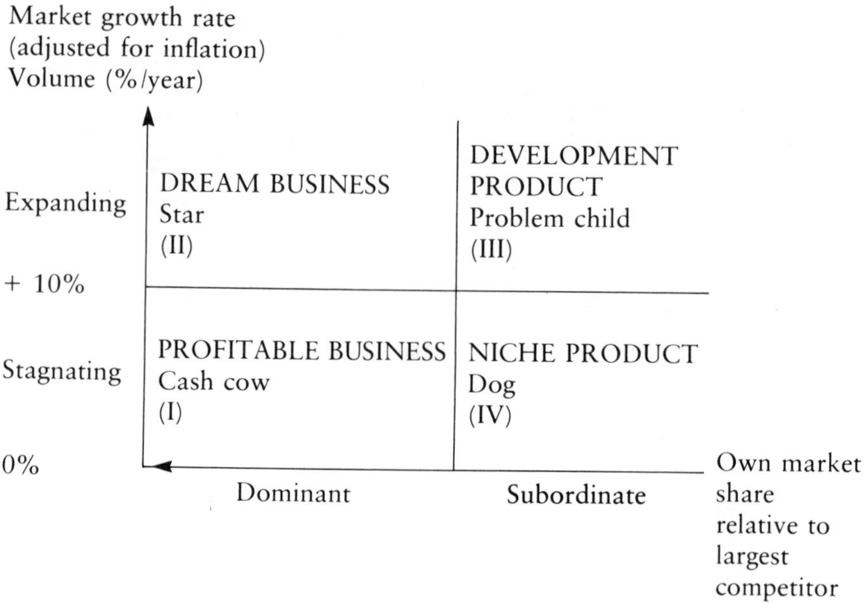

Market growth rate
(adjusted for inflation)
Volume (%/year)

	Dominant	Subordinate
Expanding + 10%	DREAM BUSINESS Star (II)	DEVELOPMENT PRODUCT Problem child (III)
Stagnating 0%	PROFITABLE BUSINESS Cash cow (I)	NICHE PRODUCT Dog (IV)

Own market share relative to largest competitor

Figure 42

In square II, we find 'star' products. These are products which are dominant in an expansive market. Very often stars do not yield so much money in this stage because of large-scale investment, but they will later when the market is stagnant. Stars then turn into cash cows.

In square III are development products which, if handled in the right way, can become stars; but this assumes a superior strategy and whole-hearted commitment to the product in question.

Square IV shows a difficult strategic situation. There is no idea of trying to become dominant in a stagnating market where we are subordinate to the competition. On the other hand, it may be an idea to try and differentiate the product and find a market niche where one can avoid confrontation with the dominant competition. Doing this can make the business profitable, if only just.

Figure 43 shows how the BCG model can be used. The arrows show the following: money earned from the (in logical terms) highly profitable cash cows is put into a selected development product, a problem child (1), so that its market share subsequently increases and it becomes a dominant product in its market—a 'star' (2). When the market slowly stagnates, the star becomes a cash cow (3).

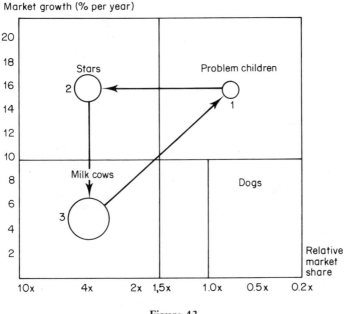

Figure 43

HONDA

Honda's strategy for conquering the world market for motorcycles, and its application of the BCG model is an example of masterly step-by-step market penetration:

(1) Honda first aimed at becoming the market leader for motorcycles in Japan, where the market was growing rapidly.
(2) The money earned when market domination in Japan had been achieved was put into the US market.
(3) Once market domination had been achieved in the US as well, they aimed at becoming the market leader in Europe and developing countries.
(4) By 1975, they had achieved their aim of becoming the market leader in all their main markets.

131

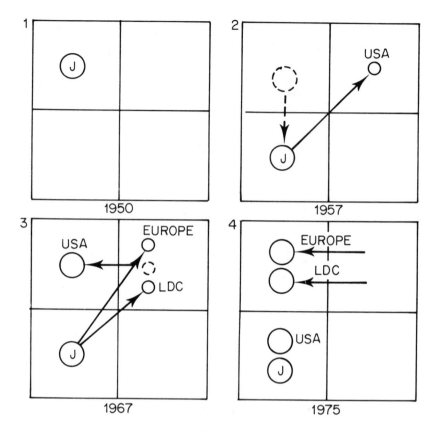

Figure 44

The BCG model can be expanded to deal with shrinking markets (Figure 45):

A shrinking market will sooner or later lead to a product being abandoned. If you have a dominant share of the market, however, the business is still profitable to start with (square VI). The position relative to the competition is very strong (hence 'warhorse'). In some cases, you may even decide that retreat is called for and that the economic situation may rapidly turn to market upswing. A languishing business with a thought-out winding-up strategy can be enormously profitable.

In box V, the only choice is to pull out as quickly as possible. This may not be so easy, however, since we are acting here from a position of weakness.

Market growth

	Dominant	Subordinate
Expanding + 10%	**Dream business** Stars (II)	**Development product** Problem child (III)
Stagnating 0%	**Profitable business** Cash cows (I)	**Niche products** Dogs (IV)
Shrinking − 10%	LANGUISHING BUSINESS 'Warhorses' (VI)	WINDING-UP PRODUCT 'Dodos'* (V)

Own relative market share

* The terms 'warhorse' and 'dodo' come from Barksdale (1982). The dodo is an extinct species of bird which could not fly and hence was completely at the mercy of its enemies.

Figure 45

Marketing warfare and the BCG model

We will now go further and apply the military methods of conflict and conflict environments to the BCG model (Figure 46).

Market growth rate

	Dominating	Subordinate
Expanding + 10%	ATTACK (Direct strategy) (II)	ATTACK (Indirect strategy) (III)
Stagnant 0%	DEFENCE (Direct/indirect strategy) (I)	ATTACK/DEFENCE/ RETREAT (Indirect strategy) (IV)
Shrinking − 10%	DEFENCE/RETREAT (Direct/indirect strategy) (VI)	RETREAT (V)

Own relative market share

Figure 46

I. High market share—low growth

This favourable strategic situation is one that should be guarded as long as possible. In military terms, we are fighting on certain terrain with a good chance of warding off enemy attacks. Much the same applies in marketing warfare. There is no reason to let go of market shares straight away. All defence strategies (except strategic retreat) are applicable. Both direct and indirect strategy can be used, even if indirect is probably the most cost-effective. Defence must be highly flexible, which means that purely positional defence is generally unsuitable. Better distribution is probably given by mobile defence, preventive attack, counter-attack or flank positional defence.

II. Large market share—high growth

This is our star case. In military terms, it can be illustrated by open terrain where we have great attacking strength and mobility against an inferior enemy. It is a question here of using classical strategy of the Napoleonic type to beat the enemy in direct attack and hence reach a decisive solution. Frontal attack is recommended if superiority is great enough. The attack should be made quickly and in great force.

III. Low market share—high growth

Only indirect attack strategies apply here. The offensive is made after careful consideration and calculated risk-taking. Elite troops are used as spearheads to prepare the market for bigger operations. High-technology niche products, mainly with in-built synergy effects, enter the market first as a bridgehead for further penetration. Surprise, accumulation of forces and freedom of action must be achieved.

IV. Low market share—low growth

In this situation, aims must be limited. Guerrilla strategy is often suitable. Indirect strategy should be used for success. If we choose to remain in the market, we must differentiate our product and find a market niche where we can avoid confrontation with the dominant competition. Do not be averse to strategic retreat, that is, selling the operation.

V. Low market share—negative growth

The only thing here is to get out as quickly as possible, that is, sell the operation.

VI. High market share—negative growth

The choice here is between positional defence and retreat. If the decision is made to defend one's position, this should not be at excessively high cost. Freedom of action to pull out or go on to the offensive must be maintained.

The eleven options discussed in Chapter 10 can therefore be placed in the BCG model as in Figure 47.

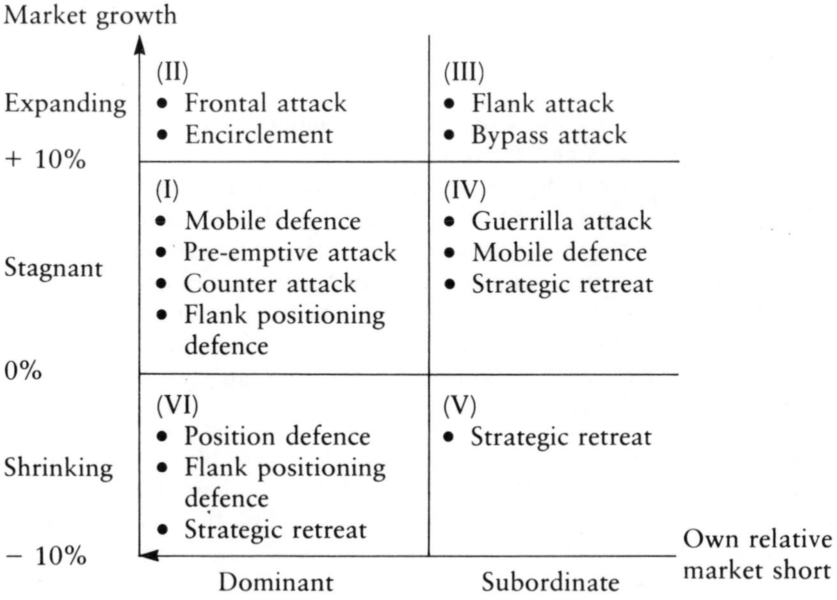

Market growth

	Dominant	Subordinate
Expanding + 10%	(II) • Frontal attack • Encirclement	(III) • Flank attack • Bypass attack
Stagnant 0%	(I) • Mobile defence • Pre-emptive attack • Counter attack • Flank positioning defence	(IV) • Guerrilla attack • Mobile defence • Strategic retreat
Shrinking − 10%	(VI) • Position defence • Flank positioning defence • Strategic retreat	(V) • Strategic retreat

Own relative market short

Figure 47

As with all models, this is obviously a simplification of reality. It cannot be ruled out, for example, that other methods of conflict may give good results in certain cases. However, it gives so much guidance that very good reason would have to exist for the choice of strategy to be made from other starting points. The model is of great use in generating and choosing options. (Cf. the strategic decision-making process, Chapter 12.)

FERMENTA AND THE BCG MODEL

Phase 1

Let us look at how Fermenta applied the Boston matrix and changed its position (Figure 48).

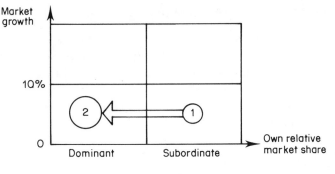

Figure 48

(1) In 1983, Fermenta was a dog in the penicillin group (that is base and medium products and active substances).
(2) By an aggressive policy of acquisition, they bought Pharmaceutical Company's operations in this (for them) unglamorous field. A company such as this had no commitment to getting raw materials for pharmaceutical preparations, but saw it only as a necessary evil. Fermenta, on the other hand, had developed advanced technology for 6-APA production, the basis of all semi-synthetic penicillins, with which they were able to improve productivity rapidly in the facilities they had purchased.

Conclusion: Through takeovers, which were made possible by an advanced production process, Fermenta had got hold of the Pharmaceutical company's 'dogs'. By putting together a whole kennel-full, they had moved up from the dog to the cash cow position. Fermenta's course of action was logical. If people want to get rid of their dogs, why not buy? The price should be quite reasonable. In this case, Fermenta used the Boston Consulting Group's general advice on dogs: buy them, do not sell them.

Phase 2

Now that Fermenta had reached the position of being a cash cow in the penicillin field, they moved into the expansive fields of cefalosporin (3), veterinary medicine (4) and feedstuff additives (5).

Through their takeovers in 1984, they acquired production equipment, market contacts and, together with new company acquisitions, managed to move from a 'problem child' to a 'star' position from 1985 to 1986. Even if

Fermenta had not managed to make this change, they would probably have had a good position since they had such well-developed synergy effects between the various operations (fighting behind the lines), and they had bought the production equipment cheaply (Figure 49).

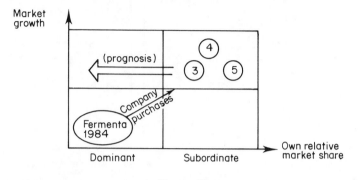

Figure 49

Conclusion: The cash cow position of the bulk of their operations enabled new and aggressive company acquisition within expanding product fields. By achieving synergy between different fields, they stopped being subordinate to the competition. In phase 2, as far as we can see, they followed BCG's general advice.

Fermenta's application of the Boston matrix shows the importance of not following system theories slavishly, and that it can sometimes be right to do something else. The most important thing is knowing what you are doing and what risks you are taking.

Note: Fermenta got into financial problems in 1986/87; not because their strategy was wrong but because it was poorly executed.

Marketing warfare and the GE model

The General Electric portfolio matrix can be used as an aid in defining strategic situations in outline terms and hence as an indication of what strategy to choose if desired. The GE product portfolio matrix looks like Figure 50.

You then put either your strategic business units (SBUs) or products as circles in the matrix, by assessing the factors which determine partly what makes a market attractive to you, partly what competitive force there is on the market. The attractiveness of the market depends amongst other things on the following factors:

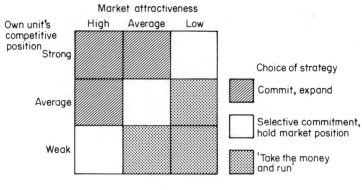

Figure 50

- Expansion rate
- Market size
- Season variations
- Customer size
- Competition intensity

- Market profitability
- Technical development
- Frequency of new products
- Legislation
- Buyer concentration

The competitive position depends on such factors as:

- Relative market share
- Market share
- R&D capacity
- Marketing costs
- Quality

- Range
- Product's position in life-cycle
- Capacity utilization
- Capital intensity

Determining market attractiveness and one's own competitive position is in most cases far too complicated, which has given the model an undeservedly poor reputation among many business leaders. As always, some simplification of reality is necessary to make the problem manageable. The important thing is to know what one is doing and what gaps this can lead to in analysis.

A typical product portfolio may look something like Figure 51: the size of the circles indicates the total market and the shaded portions our own share.

Let us now combine the Boston Consulting Group and General Electric portfolio models, which is not difficult since the BCG model can be regarded as a simplified version of the other.

We will swap the axes in the GE matrix so that market attractiveness is shown vertically (*y*-axis) and competitive position horizontally (*x*-axis), the same as in the BCG model.

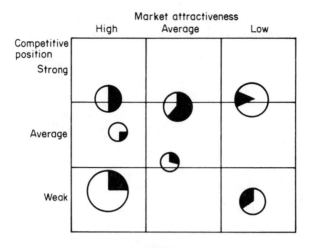

Figure 51

The *main* factor which decides whether a market is attractive is the rate at which it is expanding. Rapidly expanding markets are highly attractive. In the same way, we can say that the most important factor determining one's own competitiveness is one's relative market share. If we accept these simplifications, the BCG model can be incorporated in the GE model (Figure 52).

Market attractiveness—GE (Growth rate—BCG)	High	Stars II		Problem child III
	Average	Cash cows I		Dogs IV
	Low	Warhorse VI		Dodo V
		High	Equal	Low

Competitive position—GE
(Relative market share—BCG)

Figure 52

In this BCG/GE model, the different military strategies and environments are distributed as shown in Figure 53.

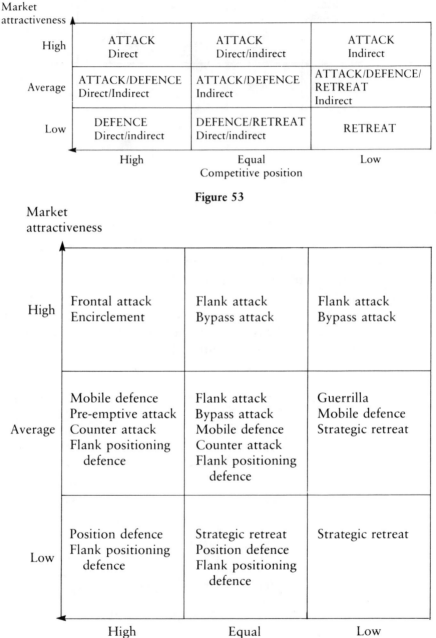

Market attractiveness

	High	Equal	Low
High	ATTACK Direct	ATTACK Direct/indirect	ATTACK Indirect
Average	ATTACK/DEFENCE Direct/Indirect	ATTACK/DEFENCE Indirect	ATTACK/DEFENCE/ RETREAT Indirect
Low	DEFENCE Direct/indirect	DEFENCE/RETREAT Direct/indirect	RETREAT

Competitive position

Figure 53

Market attractiveness

	High	Equal	Low
High	Frontal attack Encirclement	Flank attack Bypass attack	Flank attack Bypass attack

Average	Mobile defence
	Pre-emptive attack
	Counter attack
	Flank positioning
	   defence
		Flank attack
		Bypass attack
		Mobile defence
		Counter attack
		Flank positioning
		   defence
			Guerrilla
			Mobile defence
			Strategic retreat

Low	Position defence
	Flank positioning
	   defence
		Strategic retreat
		Position defence
		Flank positioning
		   defence
			Strategic retreat

Competitive position

Figure 54

In this way, we can allocate the 11 strategies discussed in Chapter 10. This gives the picture shown in Figure 54.

Different phases of the marketing war

There are great similarities between the phases of marketing warfare and those of classical warfare. Like military operations, marketing operations follow a specific life-cycle. This means that it helps to be aware of the dynamics of battle to give yourself space and time to make good decisions in marketing.

The course of military struggle can be illustrated as in Figure 55.

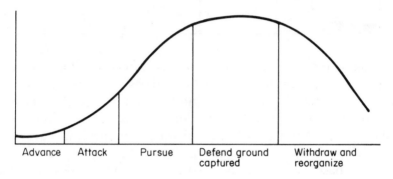

| Advance | Attack | Pursue | Defend ground captured | Withdraw and reorganize |

Figure 55

Applying this to the marketing war gives the following model shown in Figure 56.

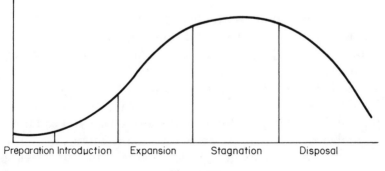

| Preparation Introduction | Expansion | Stagnation | Disposal |

Figure 56

The process is basically the same in both cases, which means that military conflict techniques can be used as a starting-point when considering which tactics should be used in the various phases of marketing operations. Let us look at each phase in turn and see what parallels we can find.

Advance/preparation

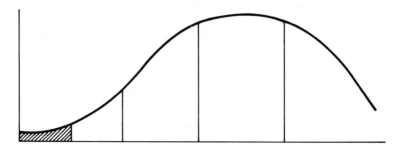

In this phase, the aim is to ensure one's own freedom of action and at the same time reduce that of the other side as much as possible. The offensive is carefully prepared. Information about the enemy is gathered and processed. Information on market requirements is produced. Alternative distribution channels and positions are established. Minor conflicts can be engaged in in the market for establishing further bases for decisions. Predictions are made, based on facts and hypotheses. Strategy is established after careful consideration. When this has been determined, the starting point for attack is occupied. At the same time, massive support is organized to ensure success in the attacking phase. Diversionary manoeuvres should also be carried out to improve the initial position still further.

Preparations should display the following characteristics:

- Careful preparations—established facts.
- Realistic analysis—not wishful thinking.
- Look for smart, cost-effective solutions—indirect strategies/ methods.
- Think first about flank attack and guerrilla strategy.
- Retain freedom of action—do not show the enemy your hand.
- If possible, design your forces and plans so that you can threaten a number of different targets—keep the enemy in the dark.
- Ensure safety—do not give the enemy the chance of attacking in this phase.

Attack/introduction

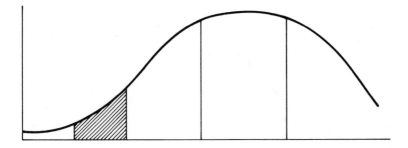

Once you have made your decision, built up your fighting potential relative to the enemy and occupied the starting position for the attack, carry through the attack with great force and decisiveness.

In this phase, you may accept an over-low selling price so as to be able to proceed quickly along the learning curve and so achieve lower unit costs than your competitors. The aim is to penetrate the enemy's lines and as quickly as possible to create a position which confronts the enemy with a foregone conclusion. Do not give the enemy the chance of fighting back unnecessarily. It is in this phase that the decisive battle will be achieved.

There are some important principles for the introductory phase:

- Create local attacks in force—if necessary with local superiority (spearhead products).
- Position your products mentally in the consciousness of customers and competitors: 'the firstest with the mostest'.
- Coordinate supporting operations and attacking movements—do whatever is needed to ensure the strength of the attacking forces.
- Keep to your aim—do not let developments influence your plans unnecessarily.
- Keep fighting spirit up—personal leadership is essential.
- Keep it simple—speed and strength are more important than finesse when plans have been selected and are being put into action.

Pursuit/expansion

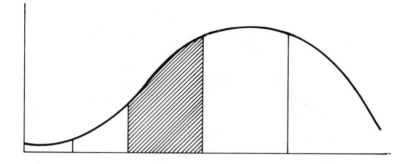

The aim is now to complete success *forcefully* within the context of the overall aim. It is for this reason that military reserves are kept. The enemy should now be thoroughly demoralized. Powerful, co-ordinated resistance should no longer be possible. Reserves are sent in to complete the success and take as much ground as possible. The aim is to create the desired market position and create the conditions for long-term success to defend it. Relative marketing costs, as well as production, purchasing and development costs will fall gradually in this phase. Profitability rises dramatically.

Principles in this phase:

- Keep the attack going—do not give the enemy room to breathe. Concentrate on advertising, salesforce training, acquiring new dealers, and so on.
- Push deep into the enemy lines and spread attack gradually—*let the entire reserve attack*. Now that we are truly established, we can spread ourselves out over the market by introducing new products in rapid succession. New geographical markets. New market sectors, new products, technological development.
- Ensure adequate security on the flanks—do not let the enemy counter-attack. Buy up complementary products, dealers, competing companies and competitors' key personnel.
- Create new mobile reserves bit by bit. Commit fresh capital to customer claims, warehousing, increased capacity, distribution systems. Be creative and entrepreneurial—be prepared to grasp opportunities which frequently happen in this phase. A high degree of sensitivity to market needs and flexibility in meeting them are important factors in increasing market penetration.

144

Defending occupied territory/stagnation

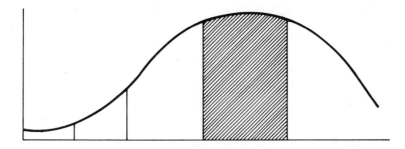

We have now achieved our aim, and must now organize our defence so that our position in the market can be held in the long term. Now we reap the rewards of our efforts. Prices can very often be set at a highly profitable level. But do not forget to keep an eye on the enemy at all times. Only then will we have control over what happens on the other side and constitute a threat which reduces the enemy's freedom of action.

The following principles apply in the stagnation phase:

- Defence strategy with a high degree of mobility—keep the enemy in the dark.
- Economize on your forces—it is here that we can now save money. Increasing cost-effectiveness, rationalization, using economies of scale, reduction of number of product variations, and so on.
- Keep up the impression of superior forces—do not give the enemy the idea of counter-attacking without comprehensive preparations and build-up of forces. Consciously build up your company's image as an incredibly effective and creative opponent.
- Beat back any attempts by the enemy at repositioning—keep a strong reserve force. Keep a watch in product areas which could be substitutes for your products. Get involved in and keep an eye on research projects in new technology, new processes, new methods of distribution so as not to be taken by surprise by more creative competitors.
- Keep up fighting spirit, even in this defensive phase—good morale is vital to keep your positions. Internal marketing is as important as external.

Pull out—disengage

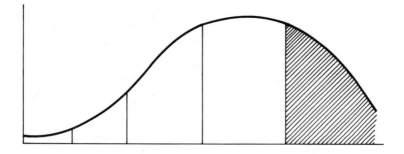

Pulling out at the right moment is a difficult art. It should be done from a position of strength and not when weaknesses are only too apparent. At the same time, disengagement should not be so early that receipts are reduced unnecessarily. The retreat should be an orderly one and should take place in parallel with other operations starting up. If parts of operations are to be disposed of, it is incredibly important that other parts should be developed so that the workforce has something positive to look forward to. Braking and accelerating at the same time is difficult but necessary. Operations should therefore be switched in orderly fashion to other future-oriented sectors.

Important principles in this phase:

- Careful preparation—set up a disengagement plan.
- Keep the enemy in ignorance of your intentions—ensure security.
- Keep a tight hold on operations—do not let retreat turn into rout.
- Keep an eye on fighting spirit—special measures will probably need to be taken to strengthen morale during this sensitive phase.

Marketing warfare and product life-cycle

The different phases in the marketing war are connected with the position of the product on the market. This means that in many cases the 11 strategic alternatives can be linked with the product life cycle in a common model (Figure 57). It should be remembered, however, that any errors in the model will be multiplied by each other and that

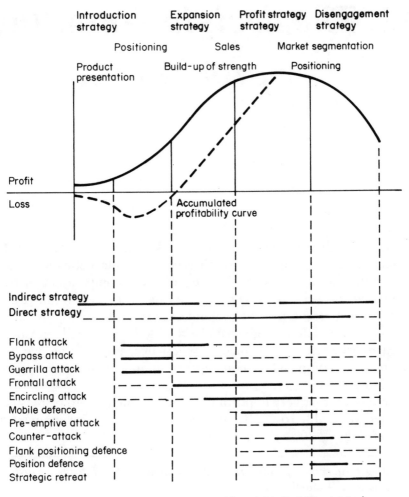

(Copyright: Durö/Sandström)

Figure 57

it is therefore necessary to be particularly critical in limiting its applicability. There is the risk of over-simplifying reality to thè point where there is no longer any purpose in using the model.

12 The decision-making process

The strategic theories which we have looked at provide the basis for strategic understanding and establishing viable marketing strategies. Further theories and models could be added to complete the picture. In our view, however, this is unnecessary in most cases. We have tried to make the presentation simple and easy to understand, and at the same time complete enough to make the model applicable in various typical market situations. In our experience, the theories we have presented are completely adequate, even in quite complicated market situations.

There is another very important problem which has to be mastered in order to be able to apply the theories well, however, namely the *methodology of strategic evaluation.*

> *Strategic success depends first and foremost on careful and realistic evaluation.* (Liddell Hart)

Strategic decision-making is a complicated process. There is no simple solution, as there would be in mathematics; this is in fact obvious, since we are dealing with the interaction of human wills.

As in any conflict between people or human organizations, there is a high degree of uncertainty involved. Human actions can only be planned and predicted within certain limits. Subjectivity, value judgements, forgetfulness and so on are all factors which, unless care is taken, can frustrate all constructive planning and decision-making.

It is to avoid the harmful effects of such irrelevant factors that some form of logical methodology is required to deal with problems in rational fashion. Such a methodology is written down in most military organizations, such as the USA's 'Estimate of the Situation', France's 'La Méthode' or our Swedish evaluation matrix.

All these methods have much in common. Even if their make-up and methods appear different at first sight, the underlying thought and, indeed, the content, are largely the same. The aim is to gather, coordinate and process available information in a logical and practical way for use as the relevant basis for decision-making.

Situations vary, of course. Sometimes problems are relatively simple and well-defined, at other times quite complex. In many instances, decisions have to be made under pressure of time. In other words, each situation is unique, which means that decision-making methodology must always be adapted to the actual problem in hand. This means that you have to be very careful as to what any situation actually demands in terms of methodology. This does not mean that methodology has no value as a working model for how one should proceed. The framework should be simplified or expanded, depending on the situation.

The stages in military decision-making are as illustrated in Figure 58.

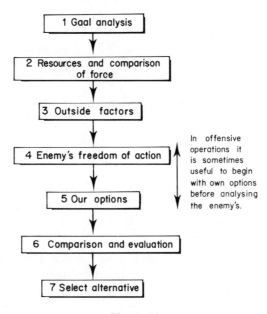

Figure 58

We will go through this decision-making process step by step, in relatively detailed fashion. First, the model is described step by step, following by an outline of the model as a whole.

If the model seems complicated, remember what we said about the necessity of adapting the methodology to actual problems. It is not our intention to claim that strategic decisions must always be made on the basis of comprehensive evaluation which goes into the most minute detail. There are examples of good strategic decisions which were apparently made without detailed evaluation having been made beforehand. Moreover, in the rare cases where viable decisions are made by chance, it is our conviction that logic and method were still the decisive factor, even if they were only at the back of the decision-makers' minds. To be intuitive or creative takes conscious or unconscious method.

> *The victorious general will have made a careful evaluation in good time before the battle. The loser gave little thought before the battle.* (Sun Tzu)

Goal analysis

The start of any decision-making process is setting the goal, that is, what the strategy is supposed to achieve. This also ties in with the first principle of warfare: set a goal and keep to it.

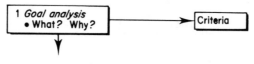

Figure 59

Where tactics are concerned, goal analysis can often be carried out by clarifying the orders given from higher up the command chain. Where strategy is concerned, the goal must be established and the situation as a whole analysed.

When an order is received (pre-set goal), it is always useful to begin the analysis by looking at the order in literal terms. In this way, one can ensure that all those who may need to be involved in the decision get a clear picture of the basis. If the goal is established after analysing an order, the aim of this analysis is to establish what the

150

overall leader *wants* to be carried out and *why* he wants that and nothing else. The overall situation is also analysed to the extent needed to clarify these two starting-points.

Once the aim has been established and people are clear as to what is to be achieved and why, one should also list the value criteria which will later be used in decision-making to evaluate alternative strategies. Examples of such criteria are:

- limitations on freedom to manoeuvre in all conflicts;
- priorities;
- time scale;
- what it is desirable to do in the long term.

Remember: Set your goal in view of the situation as a whole. Clarify what you want to do and why. Make the requisite *assumptions* as a basis for ongoing work.

Resources and comparing strengths

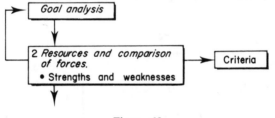

Figure 60

The aim of this stage is to establish our own and the enemy's strengths and weaknesses in various respects. This analysis looks at the numbers and types of our own and the enemy's forces (fighting potential). This is the most objective section of the decision-making process; but it cannot be sufficiently emphasized that it must take account of the preceding goal analysis. It should not therefore be restricted to a purely numerical exercise, but the possibilities in *time* and *space* must be established. Never be afraid to use the question 'is it important?' to test the importance of the various facts presented.

It is also important at all times to evaluate qualitative differences and what they involve. It is just such differences which will later lead to the formation of viable alternatives. The results of the comparison of forces also provide the basis for further criteria which can later be used in evaluating the various alternatives.

151

There is not always sufficient knowledge of the enemy's resources at the time decisions are made. Uncertainty can sometimes be so great that one is forced to make assumptions about the enemy's forces. Such assumptions must not only take his forces characteristics into account; under some circumstances, it is also necessary to speculate as to his intentions.

Remember: Decide the characteristics of both sides' forces. Compare these characteristics and look for *strengths* and *weaknesses*. Make further *assumptions* if necessary. Make the examination *goal-oriented*.

Outside factors

The environment, that is, the surroundings in which forces act, may have a great influence on available options. It is therefore important to analyse the effects of these factors carefully; but the analysis must not be limited to geography or the weather, but must also take account of political, economic and psychological factors.

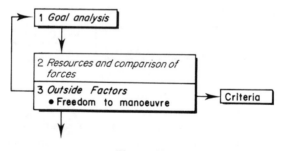

Figure 61

As in the previous stage, this should be done in a goal-oriented fashion. Only factors which affect the performance of the task should be included.

Remember: *establish* how your own and the enemy's options are affected by outside factors. Make the evaluation *goal-oriented*.

The enemy's options

The next step is to assess the options open to the enemy.

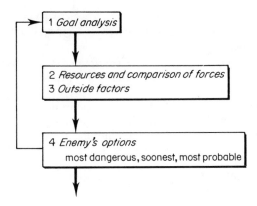

Figure 62

These are considered from the enemy's viewpoint and handled and evaluated on that basis. An enemy option in this sense means an action which the enemy is capable of carrying out in purely physical terms and which would seriously affect our task. The basic data for the production of these options are taken from earlier resource inventories. It should be pointed out that enemy options are produced objectively, that is, without taking account of how our actions could affect them. The result of these deliberations should be a *broad spectrum* of what the enemy is capable of doing and how these options then affect our freedom to manoeuvre. Analysing the enemy's options should show what is *most dangerous* to us, but also what is seen as *probable* and what can happen *soon*.

An example of how the enemy's options can be generated is given by the following model:

(1) Assume what different *aims* the enemy may have.	AIM 1		AIM 2	
(2) What *main methods* can the enemy use for reaching these aims?	METHOD 1.1	METHOD 1.2	METHOD 2.1	
(3) What different *options* does the enemy have of using his resources?	OPTION 1.1.1	OPTION 1.1.2	OPTION 1.2.1	OPTION 2.1.1

153

(4) *Select options*—not less than 2, and not more than 4 reasonable options (or combinations of options) which are *basically different*. In this way, we create the framework for the enemy's actions.	ENEMY OPTION 1	ENEMY OPTION 2	ENEMY OPTION 3
	The selected options take the form of reasonable **hypotheses** on his actions.		
	Each option is given time, force and space conditions in the short term and outlined in the long term and the main **weaknesses** for the enemy.		

In the marketing war, this model might then look like this:

(1) What are the competitor's aims?	1 Increase his profit margin	2 Increase his volume
(2) What main methods can they use to reach their aims?	1.1 Better product at higher price	2.1 Larger market share through reduced price
	1.2 Lower manufacturing costs	2.2 Larger market share through harder marketing
(3) What are their options?	1.1.1 Other material of lower weight	2.1.1 Price war
	1.1.2 New technical function	2.1.2 Cheaper components in products
	1.2.1 Automated production	2.2.1 Tigher sales network
	1.2.2 Production in low-wage countries	2.2.2 Complementing with new distribution channels
	1.2.3 Cheaper components in products	
(4) Select options	ALTERNATIVE 1 Better product at higher price through other material with lower weight (Time/space conditions? Weaknesses?)	ALTERNATIVE II Larger market share through harder marketing by tighter sales network and complemented by new distribution channels (Time/space conditions? Weaknesses?)

Once you have established hypotheses about the competition, we have created the basis for evaluating and selecting our own strategy. It is also time to direct intelligence gathering with the aim of monitoring the hypotheses and giving an early indication of which option the competition has chosen.

Remember: Draw up an inventory of the enemy's options. Classify these options in terms of the type of task, planning level, time and information received and in terms of the *degree of risk*, *probability* and what can happen *soonest*.

Our options

Now it is time to look at our own options (conceivable strategies). These must be drawn up in such a way as to establish the whole spectrum of possible strategies. In other words, alternatives established must be so all-inclusive that as far as possible no relevant alternative will be overlooked in the treatment.

As with the enemy's options, working out our own options requires a great deal of imagination and ability to tune into the actual situation. The first thing to do before starting to work out options is to go back to the goal analysis to that you are certain that the options relate to that. In the same way, analysis of our own forces and their capabilities should be repeated anew. Then alternatives can be produced and listed (Figure 63).

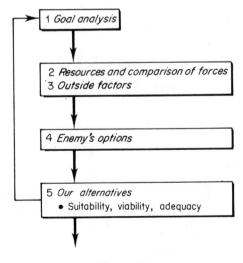

Figure 63

In a relevant list of alternatives:

- the alternatives meet the goal;
- they are comparable;
- they cover the spectrum of conceivable strategies;
- two or more options can be carried out at the same time;
- none of the options can be rejected.

A logical and relevant list of options is a precondition for being able to choose a viable alternative methodically in the next stage. A great deal of trouble should therefore be taken over this important step.

Once our options have been listed and set out as fully as possible, it is time to evaluate them overall. The aim of this evaluation is to remove less interesting options and leave only those which are considered to offer a high degree of effectiveness at reasonable cost.

Remember: Take *another look* at the aims and your own capabilities. Make a *complete* list of possible options. Test them for *suitability*, *viability* and *adequacy* in view of the goal. Keep interesting options (2–4) for final consideration.

Comparison of our options and the enemy's

This comparison, also commonly called the 'confrontation', is the heart of the whole decision-making process. This is without doubt the most important step in the process, since the outcome decides what strategy will finally be chosen.

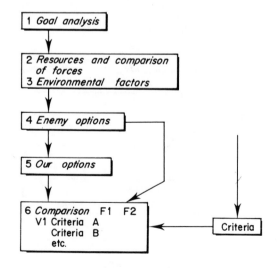

Figure 64

The confrontation aims at testing each and every one of our options against each enemy option. This is in effect a small 'wargame study', where we try and predict the outcome of each confrontation and evaluate the result.

To enable us to evaluate each confrontation in a uniform fashion, we will use the evaluation criteria listed above under decision-making. In this way, we reduce the risk of over-valuing options produced intuitively.

To gain a clear view of the confrontation and reduce the risk of anything being left out in treatment, it may be useful to apply a matrix in which the outcome of the various combinations is recorded.

Our option \ Enemy option	I	II	III
1 Criterion a Criterion b Criterion c	Assessment	Assessment	Assessment
2 Criterion a Criterion b Criterion c	Assessment	Assessment	Assessment
3 Criterion a Criterion b Criterion c	Assessment	Assessment	Assessment

Figure 65

In the assessment columns, we write in the assessment of the options in relation to the criteria in the light of the confrontation with each of the enemy options.

Remember: Go back to your decision and create useful *assessments* as a uniform evaluation standard. Confront *each and every one* of your options with *each and every one* of the enemy's. Make the assessment from *your* viewpoint.

Choosing options

Using the final result of the confrontation, logical choice of an option becomes possible. In military organizations, this choice is always the *leader's decision*, and the responsibility for it lies with him and no-one else. His staff will provide the basis for the decision and recommend an option, but it is the leader who makes the decision and his experience which decides the final choice of strategy.

In military organisations, the leader takes the decision after the requisite consideration and staff preparation. The decision is called the OVERALL DECISION, and provides the basis for further activities of troops and staff.

We can now summarize the decision-making process as in Figure 66.

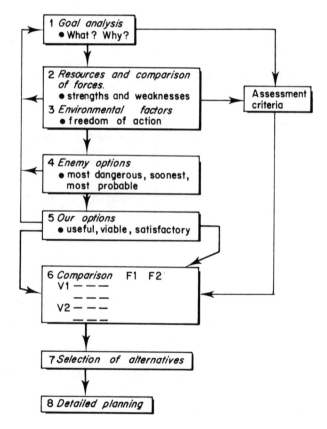

Figure 66

As was pointed out earlier, the model must be taken for what it is, a simplified model for strategic consideration and decision-making. It may need to be expanded or reduced depending on the type of strategic decision.

Strategic decision-making is complicated and difficult. We are continually having to make decisions under uncertain conditions, often under pressure of time and where poor decisions may have disastrous consequences. It is therefore important that our methods are good. Military decision-making is one such method. Applying it correctly can help us analyse strategic problems and lead us to viable solutions. But it is also important to remember that this is only an aid, a model, a way of ordering our thoughts. It can never replace the thoughts themselves.

> *The excellent general weighs the situation before he moves. He does not blunder aimlessly into baited traps. He is prudent, but not hesitant. He realizes that there are 'some roads not to be followed, some armies not to be attacked, some cities not to be besieged, some positions not to be contested and some commands of the sovereign not to be obeyed'. He takes calculated risks but never needless ones. He does not 'beard a tiger or rush a river without caring whether he lives or dies'. When he sees opportunity he acts swiftly and decisively. (Sun Tzu)*

13 Tomorrow's marketing strategy

In their book *In Search of Excellence*, Peters and Waterman claim that successful strategy has its basis in psychological advantage. By the same token, this is the heart of the matter in all strategy. Success in warfare has always been based on superior morale, which in turn is very often based on a better understanding than the enemy of the nature of the conflict of wills.

Success in marketing goes to whoever knows how to use their forces and who can see and use weaknesses in the competition. Ongoing customer strategy is at the root of success. We must ensure customers get what they want and also try to convince them that it is important to choose *our* product. This self-evident fact, however, is not enough for success in the marketing war.

To achieve success, it is necessary to take action against the competition. Both internal and lateral manoeuvres are needed. In-direct methods are recommended. The outside world must be influenced so that our freedom of action remains as great as possible, at the same time as that of the competition is controlled and inhibited. Marketing warfare therefore includes lateral strategy in the form of competition strategy as well as the obvious customer strategy.

Our own strength is built up effectively by positioning and good product development, but it is just as important (if not more so) for our organization to have the necessary morale. To achieve this, an internal strategy is required which aims at getting everybody in the organization to pull together. The company's employees must in their hearts and souls know the company's values and the goals of its strategy.

Viable strategies are not achieved by accident. Analysis, method and logic are required. Bureaucracy and dithering must be avoided. The equation undoubtedly needs the right man to bring it together. Although simplicity should be one of our guidelines, there are no simple solutions in observing that strategic decisions should be simple. Our models do not solve problems, but are a useful aid in solving them. Experience of war gives the proof of this. Bismarck is supposed to have said, 'Fools say that they learn from their mistakes. I prefer to learn from those of others.'

The struggle in the marketplace is in principle no different from any other form of struggle. There is therefore every reason to use military experience in the marketing war. Unnecessary mistakes are not only costly—they can be disastrous.

Tomorrow's marketing strategy must be highly competition-oriented. Victory will be achieved by long-term psychological action against the competition. Short-term tactical success is no substitute for poor strategy.

Viable strategies for marketing warfare can be produced in the following way:

Figure 67

This model, which we have built up with the aid of military strategic methods in combination with traditional methods of market analysis in business, we call *Battle*.

Battle therefore stands for a logical and methodical method of establishing and carrying out viable strategies for *long-term* success. *Battle* is used to profuce plans for beating the competition. The principles are the same at any level in a company. *Battle* can be used in everyday operations at tactical/operational level, but also to illuminate a company's overall strategy.

14 Conclusion

At first sight, the aim and contents of this book may appear destructive and warlike; but nothing could be more wrong than to read our message in this way. We have tried to illustrate market forces with the aid of classical military strategy, not with the aim of propagating violent and brutal solutions but rather to show how intelligence and creativity can triumph over brute force.

The importance we have attached to psychology and indirect strategy shows the ways in which we regard our main alternatives when considering alternative attack strategies.

Success in marketing warfare goes to those who:

- grasp and master the psychological interaction between the various parties on the market;
- know how to take the initiative and act aggressively;
- who thereby meet the need for surprise, accumulation of forces and freedom to manoeuvre;
- who have sufficient fighting spirit to withstand the enemy's attacks.

Strategic action must be marked by simplicity and carefulness in planning and execution.

To some extent, it is always possible to 'muddle through', but remember that 'costly, haphazard solutions are very often a sign of mediocrity', to quote Ingvar Kamprad, chairman of the Board at IKEA.

References

(1) Beaufre, André (1902–75). French general and military theoretician. Beaufre wrote a number of important books on strategy, including nuclear strategy. His best work is possibly *Introduction à la stratégie*.

(2) Clausewitz, Carl von (1780–1831). Prussian general and military theorist. Head of the War Academy in Berlin 1818–30. Clausewitz' best work is *Vom Kriege* (*On War*), published in 1834, after his death. In this book Clausewitz developed theories of strategy which even now play an important part in the art of war.

(3) Liddell Hart, Sir Basil (1895–1970). British military theoretician. Liddell Hart started as an officer in the British army, but was badly wounded in the First World War and left active service with the rank of captain. He was possibly the foremost theorist of modern times in the field of strategy. He wrote a large number of works, of which *Strategy: The Indirect Approach* is probably the best known. He was one of the first to perceive the revolutionary effect of tank troops and attack planes on warfare.

(4) Sun Tzu wrote *The Art of War*, the first important textbook of military strategy, over 2000 years ago. The theses of this classic work are still valid. In his foreword to a modern edition (Oxford University Press, New York, 1963), Liddell Hart wrote that this book is the best introduction one could imagine to the art of war and is no less valuable for intensive study.

(5) Kotler, Philip and Singh, Ravi wrote a noted article on 'Marketing warfare' in the *Journal of Business Strategy* (winter 1981), which provides a good basis for applying the principles of warfare to comprehensible business strategies.

(6) Ries, Al and Trout, Jack published a book, *Positioning: the Battle for Your Mind* (McGraw-Hill Book Company, New York 1980), which describes market positioning and can be said to be one of the best-sellers in terms of building up fighting strength in the marketing war.

(7) Peters, Thomas J. and Waterman Jr., Robert A. wrote *In Search of Excellence* (Harper & Row, New York, 1982), which attracted a great deal of attention. The book deals with the secrets behind the most successful American companies.

(8) In 1981, a strategic study was developed at the Swedish Military Academy by lecturers working there (Hugemark, Persson, Rahme, Rossander, Sandström). Among other things, this study looks at theories of the future in a somewhat new and revolutionary way.

(9) Sobel, Robert, his two books, *IBM–Colossus in Transition* (Times Books), and *Car Wars* (a Truman Talley Book) are very well written, interesting and particularly worth reading for company heads in the computer and car industries.

(10) Ohmae, Kenichi, his book *Triad Power* (The Free Press) is a detailed description, perhaps a little frightening, of why the major multinations work with their competitors in other parts of the world. A 'must' for heads of multinational companies.